The Age of Killer Robots

By: Abishur Prakash

To those who fight for peace.

This book was edited by artificial intelligence (AI).

Life Disclaimer

This book has a finite lifespan. The rate at which killer robots are advancing, and the number of new developments taking place, mean that within a short period of time, this book will be irrelevant.

Table of Contents

Dictionary

Artificial Intelligence (AI): There are three broad categories that explain how AI is expected to evolve:

- **Artificial Narrow Intelligence (ANI):** An AI system that can function with some degree of human intelligence.
- **Artificial General Intelligence (AGI):** An AI system that can match all aspects of human intelligence.
- **Artificial Super Intelligence (ASI):** An AI system that exceeds human intelligence.

AI Chips: Semiconductors designed to handle artificial intelligence processes. Certain chips provide military robots with even greater capabilities.

Automated Military: The replacement of humans with robots and artificial intelligence to bring down military costs but still maintain military strength and capabilities.

Autonomous Weapons: Autonomous means acting on its own. Autonomous weapons are a technical term for killer robots. There are three categories of autonomous weapons:

- First, there are **fully-autonomous weapons**, which can make decisions without humans.
- Second, there are **semi-autonomous weapons**, which have autonomous

capabilities but are under human control most of the time.

- Third, there are military robots which **could have autonomous capabilities** in the future, such as battlefield robots that are remotely controlled by soldiers.

Cyborg Soldiers: Human soldiers that have technology integrated into their body. The integrated technology may act autonomously to protect the soldier and enhance capabilities.

Military-Civil Fusion: This is a bridge between the military and civil spheres to transfer and share knowledge in order to develop more advanced technologies and capabilities.

Multi-Robot Communication: The systems that allow robots to work in a team, act autonomously and communicate with each other to carry out tasks and objectives. This is different from a swarm because, traditionally, a swarm encompasses a single type of robot, such as a drone. Multi-robot communication involves different types of robots, such as an autonomous tank, drones and helicopter.

Robots: A machine or system that can replicate human tasks. Robots can be physical or digital.

Swarm Intelligence: The underlying technology behind robot swarms. It allows robots to operate and communicate with each other.

UGV: UGV stands for **unmanned ground vehicle**. This is a vehicle that is controlled remotely or operates autonomously based on pre-programmed rules and parameters.

UAV: UAV stands for **unmanned aerial vehicle.** This is a technical term for drones. They operate without any human on board. Traditionally, UAVs are remotely controlled. However, increasingly these drones are gaining autonomous capabilities.

UUV: UUV stands for **unmanned underwater vehicle.** This is a type of drone that operates without any humans on board. Increasingly, these vessels are autonomous but are not armed (yet).

UCAV: UGV, UAV and UUV have been traditionally non-combat. Now, governments are developing these vehicles with combat in mind. These vehicles have combat added to their name, such as Unmanned Combat Aerial Vehicle (UCAV).

Introduction

For all of history, humans have fought one another.

First, the fights involved food or shelter. Then, it was over land or resources. As fights evolved into wars, the weapons changed. Swords and spears became bombs and bayonets. Then, machine guns and missiles. But, regardless of the war, or the reason for the war, the implications of war never changed. One side lost people, the other side gained new prisoners. One side grew their power, the other side lost their power. One empire was created, another empire was destroyed.

In short, each war changed the balance of power in the world.

Throughout history, while tools and tactics changed, warfare always revolved around humans. This is the "model of warfare" that has existed, not just for decades or centuries, but since the beginning of the human species. It is a model that puts humans at the center.

It is humans that fight wars and also start wars.

But, now, a new model is emerging. And, it takes humans out of the center. In their place is a technology that is unfamiliar and unprecedented. It goes by many names, such as "lethal autonomous weapons systems" or

LAWS. But, there is a simpler and more commonly used name for this technology. It is called "killer robots."

Killer robots represent the biggest shift in warfare.

They are machines and systems that operate autonomously, without human input or control. They are able to identify and engage targets, including people, all on their own. It means that an autonomous drone can attack targets without human approval or a swarm of armed, autonomous tanks can carry out missions on their own.

For the first time, the military power of a nation will no longer be fully controlled by humans. It will also be controlled by advanced, sophisticated artificial intelligence (AI) - the brains of killer robots.

Soon, it may be killer robots that fight wars - and killer robots that start wars.

This new future has huge ramifications for the world. It has the potential to bring about chaos, complexity and confusion. It can greatly transform the geopolitical landscape and alter the future world history. And, there is little that can be done to stop it.

The following pages are an exploration of the new kind of challenges and shifts that killer robots could create. This book goes beyond the infamous "terminator complex," whereby killer robots could take over the world and threaten the human race. Instead, this book is an exploration of the new and undiscussed issues surrounding killer robots. For example, what kind of ethics should killer robots have? Or, how might killer robots challenge political rights and freedoms in a society?

As one reads this book, they should do so not by comparing it to the past but by discarding the past. There is no precedent for killer robots. Do not look to the 1950s to understand how an autonomous missile defense system might think. Such technology has never existed before. To look at killer robots, is essentially, to accept a future that has no equivalent in history.

For the first time, militaries will have technology that is superior to humans in all aspects. The tank or fighter jet may have been superior to humans in its ability to inflict physical damage or move faster, but it did not have the intelligence that humans had. Humans still had to be at the helm of both vehicles. This is not the case with killer robots. Every killer robot will be exponentially more capable and intelligent than a human being (or team of human beings).

There are seven chapters in this book, each exploring a different dimension of killer robots.

The first chapter looks at the immediate challenges that nations will be faced with if their killer robots make a decision, such as attacking another country. The behavior of killer robots will "jolt" governments and this could push them into dangerous territory.

The second chapter explores the ethics of killer robots, and the kind of ethics that nations could install into killer robots to make them behave a certain way. It also looks at the challenges of ethics, and how ethics could lead to certain kinds of behavior, and tensions between countries.

The third chapter discusses what kind of rules governments and institutions should create to regulate how killer robots are traded. It also proposes a new paradigm for trading in killer robots.

The fourth chapter presents brand new possibilities that could emerge as killer robots make their way around the world. These possibilities could fundamentally alter what nations can do and how the world views killer robots in the first place.

The fifth chapter looks at ways to control killer robots as they operate around the world. And, it proposes ways to ensure killer robots understand what they have done.

The sixth chapter examines how killer robots could transform the design of militaries and societies. It also deals with how killer robots could change the balance of power in the world.

The seventh, and final chapter, looks at the infamous "terminator complex," whereby killer robots could attack humanity or cause the destruction of the human race.

Also, at the end of this book, following the conclusion, is a list of the most important organizations across the world that are fully or partly responsible for killer robots. It is intended to help defense officials, heads of state, business executives and policy makers understand who may be responsible for designing, developing or directing the field of killer robots.

At the end of the day, the impact that killer robots may or may not have on the world remains to be seen. Like with other technological revolutions, be it the Internet or electricity, there was no crystal ball to predict the immense change that followed - both positive and negative. Perhaps, killer robots will bring about immense peace in the world as the threat of them taking action deters nations from unleashing them. Or, perhaps, killer robots will bring about the next major conflict, as nations "outsource" their military and its actions to unpredictable and unfamiliar machines.

In either case, killer robots are here. Their grand entrance is moments away. The revolution is about to begin. And yet, the world knows little to nothing about them and what is possible.

It is time to change that.

Chapter One - Rude Awakening
Killer robots will force countries to pick a side

Jakarta, Indonesia
2028

In 2026, the Indonesian military deploys 50 autonomous warships, purchased from the United Kingdom (UK). These warships are unarmed. They are tasked with patrolling Indonesian waters and blocking enemy ships from coming too close to the Indonesian coast.

The moment Indonesia does this, several neighboring countries object. They warn that the Indonesian warships pose a serious security threat. However, Indonesia ignores their objections and continues with its deployment.

Over the next several months, the warships block almost 150 attempts by enemy vessels to enter Indonesian waters. Astonished by the success of these ships, Indonesia decides to take its autonomous warships to the next level.

In 2028, Indonesia gives all 50 autonomous warships advanced weapons. And, it gives artificial intelligence (AI), on board the warships, control of the weapons. In other words, the warships can decide who to attack and how - without any human input.

Shortly after doing this, the Indonesian warships encounter warships coming from Vietnam. The Indonesian warships have never encountered Vietnamese warships before. As the Indonesian warships analyze the Vietnamese ships, AI onboard the Indonesian ships begins to collate data a certain way. It predicts that the Vietnamese warships are on their way to block energy supplies of Indonesia in the South China Sea. And, that this could lead to an economic downturn in Indonesia.

The AI, tasked with protecting Indonesia, fires on the Vietnamese warships. Within minutes, three Vietnamese warships and 10 support vessels are destroyed.

It takes just a few seconds for the news to travel to Jakarta and Hanoi.

The Indonesian government begins to panic. The Indonesian president calls his Vietnamese counterpart to apologize. Except, Vietnam ignores the call. At the same time, Vietnam bans all trade with Indonesia and expels all Indonesian diplomats. On top of all this, the Association of Southeast Asian Nations (ASEAN) suspends Indonesia's membership, excluding it from the free trade market.

As these steps are taken, Indonesia's government realizes the magnitude of what has happened. Indonesia is experiencing a huge fallout, not because of anything a human has done, but because of what a killer robot has done.

And now, the country as a whole must bear the brunt of the decisions made by its killer robots.

Introduction

In October 2007, at a military training camp outside Cape Town, South Africa, a "robot cannon" fired on its own, killing nine South African soldiers and injuring 14 others. The robot cannon was an anti-aircraft weapon that had an "automatic mode," allowing it to take data from a separate unit and fire on its own. Reports of why the robot cannon fired the way it did differ. Some blame a mechanical malfunction. But, other reports blame a "computer glitch."

If it was the latter, then the events that took place at the military training camp in South Africa represent a new kind of warfare. In this kind of warfare, humans are no longer in the driver's seat, killer robots are. These robots will be making decisions and humans will be playing catch up.

In one way, South Africa got lucky, as the robot cannon was in a military training camp. Besides the unfortunate deaths and injuries of soldiers, there was no geopolitical component. Imagine what would have happened if South Africa had deployed the same robot cannon on its borders, and it had fired, on its own, at soldiers from Zimbabwe or Namibia. Things could have escalated very quickly and the outcome may have been different.

As nations around the world acquire killer robots, they must start planning for what might happen once their killer robots make a decision. In the past, governments had to deal with the fallout of human soldiers behaving a certain way. But now, alongside human behavior, is the behavior of killer robots. Countries and defense companies will be reacting and responding to what killer robots are doing - on land, in air or at sea. There is another way to put this. For the first time, countries and companies will be forced to deal with how an autonomous military technology is behaving on the world stage. This is a paradigm that the world does not have much experience with.

The next Israel-Iran conflict, started by killer robots

In the UK, a defense firm has built a drone called "Taranis," named after the Celtic god of thunder. The firm does not have plans to sell this drone. Instead, it built Taranis to "inspire" the next-generation of drones and show what they could do.

Like many other military drones, Taranis is armed and controlled by a human operator. But, unlike other drones, Taranis also has an "autonomous mode." This mode allows the drone to "think for itself" and carry out missions. In fact, Taranis was developed, in part, because of the need to have "autonomous strike" capabilities in the future.[1] [2]

As nations acquire Taranis-type drones, and deploy them, it could throw governments into situations they never imagined or are prepared for.

One country that may have Taranis-type drones is Israel. Why? Because, Israel is already a world leader when it comes to integrating drones into its military. In November 2017, a senior figure in Israel's military said that by 2030, one-third of the Israel Defense Forces (IDF) could be unmanned.[3]

And, because of volatility near Israel's borders, such as rocket or mortar fire, Israel may use armed drones as a new line of defense, alongside its various missile defense systems. In areas where humans may be too slow to react, the drones may be put into autonomous mode.

This means that the drones, tasked with protecting Israel, would be operating free of human control or input.

Could these drones exacerbate, or even start, conflicts?

For example, in February 2018, an Iranian drone tried to enter Israeli territory. Israel shot it down. According to the Israeli government, the drone was armed. This incident only added to the ongoing tensions between Israel and Iran. But, it did not result in Israel or Iran attacking each another.

But, imagine if Israel's autonomous drones were present at the time. What might have happened?

Perhaps, Israel's drones would have intervened, and attacked the Iranian drone - business as usual. But, then the drones may have gone one step further. Using data from social media, satellites and intelligence agencies, the Israeli drones may have predicted that Iran is going to launch another attack on Israel within the next 48 to 72 hours. With this prediction, the Israeli drones may then have created a new mission for themselves.

Consider what this means. A team of autonomous drones may have created their own mission, complete with who to attack and when, without any human input. Equally important is this: autonomous drones may propose (or make) life threatening decisions, in realtime and without emotions. These may be decisions that humans would only propose in very extreme cases - or perhaps, never at all.

Will Israel have programmed its drones to seek human approval before making "certain" decisions? If not, it means the Israeli drones have carte blanche - unlimited power and authority. In the past, when tensions between Israel and Iran grew, Israel attacked Iranian-proxy groups stationed in Lebanon, Iraq or Syria. But, the autonomous drones may be thinking differently. Because the Iranian drone may have tried to attack Israel directly, hence, the Israeli drones may also decide to attack Iran directly.

If the Israeli drones attack Iran, or try to attack, a global crisis will emerge. Will Iran declare war in response? What role will countries like the US, Russia, China and India play? What will happen to oil and the global economy? How will Israel respond to what its drones did? As the entire world prepares for a new war in the Middle East, for the first time, the catalyst for all of it would have been autonomous, Taranis-style drones operating tens of thousands of feet in the air and making decisions on their own.

This is the biggest risk of killer robots. They could make decisions that lead to a real and dangerous conflict. And, when governments find out what their killer robots have done, they may be in a state of shock.

Supporting or disavowing killer robots

The key question in front of countries using killer robots is this: once their killer robots make a decision, will they support or disavow what the killer robots have done?

The way nations answer this question will decide whether tensions rise or if nations are brought back from the brink of war. This has global implications.

If nations support what their killer robots have done, it means they are accepting the consequences too.

In the case of Israel and Iran, there are many ways the Israeli government may respond to what its drones have done. For example, Israel may support the drones and their decisions. This would create a new global precedent. It would mean that for the first time, autonomous systems are driving warfare - and governments are in alignment with this.

Except, if Israel comes out in support of its drones, it raises the chances of war in the Middle East. It means that Israel is supporting the attack on Iran, and Iran may view this as more justification to retaliate militarily. And, if

Israel has autonomous drones, it may be possible that Iran does too. Could Iran program its drones to target Israel? Or, if Iran's drones are fully autonomous might they automatically retaliate and attack Israel?

There is also the role that other countries will play. Every nation with a stake in the Middle East will have to decide whether they support the behavior of Israel's drones or not. There is another way of putting this. Every country with a stake in the Middle East will have to decide whether they support killer robots. The military powers like the US, Russia, China, India and others will have to fundamentally think about their support or condemnation of Israel in the age of killer robots. Can the US stand by Israel if Israeli killer robots are shifting geopolitics too much? Or, can Russia continue to stay neutral in certain issues involving Israel after killer robots are used? At the same time, countries like India, China and Japan, that depend heavily on oil imports from the Middle East - especially those that travel through the Strait of Hormuz - will have to play a role in either de-escalating tensions or picking a side to support. Can India build a real relationship with Israel if Israeli killer robots are threatening Indian oil supplies via a conflict with Iran? Or, can China truly invest in Iran if Israeli killer robots are threatening a full-scale war and Iran's future?

Alongside countries are institutions, such as the United Nations (UN) and the Shanghai Cooperation Organization (SCO). Both of these institutions will play a direct role if Israel attacks Iran through autonomous drones. But, even if these groups pass rulings and condemn the killer robots, it will only heighten global tensions. For example, what if the UN partially blames Iran for the attack by Israeli drones? They might say that Israel's drones had evidence of a future attack by Iran. At the same time, the SCO might fully condemn Israel, saying that Iran is the victim. This means that two global institutions are ruling in opposite directions. This will create more division over killer robots. And, in all of this uncertainty, and opposition, the gravity of what Israel's drones have done may be lost.

On the other hand, disavowing what killer robots have done does not mean war is averted and peace will follow.

Disavowing only creates the opportunity for deescalation. If Israel comes out and completely disavows what its killer robots did, apologizing to Iran and offering a "meeting" to resolve all issues, a regional war in the Middle East might be averted.

But, equally possible is that Iran may reject Israel's apology, and take its own action. In fact, Iran may view the autonomous drone attack as the "final straw," and may take radical actions towards Israel and its allies. Even if this is not military action, it may take other forms. For example, Iran is currently an emerging power in nano-medicines (medicines developed by nanotechnology). In the coming years, Iran may have developed extremely advanced nano-medicines for conditions like dementia, cancer or arthritis. Could Tehran refuse to export these medicines to Israel and its allies as punishment? Or, will Iran ban its pharmaceutical companies from partnerships with businesses from Israel or Israel's allies? This may not seem like a powerful reaction today, especially considering there are already sanctions that ban foreign companies from operating/investing in Iran. But in the future, when Iran has technology that the rest of the world wants, the way the world deals with Iran - including sanctions - may change. If this happens, Iran may be in a power position, and it may decide who can use its nano-medicines. Those who have been friends of Iran, may have unlimited access. And those who have been enemies, may be cast out to the wind.

When disavowing, there are other consequences to think about as well.

For example, if Israel disavows what its autonomous drones have done, then its image will change. Instead of being viewed as a responsible, mature nation who has control over its military, Israel would be viewed as a country that cannot control its own military and disagrees with its own defense policies. No nation wants to be seen as a "child" or "irresponsible" in the eyes of the world, and then be treated as such.

At the same time, whether or not Israel supports or disavows what its autonomous drones have done, countries around the world may rush to purchase killer robots. They may view what happened between Israel and Iran as the beginning of a new era of warfare. And, they may view killer robots as key to their defense and national security. In other words, the moment killer robots are used in the world, it may kickstart a global rush to acquire a technology that could create more volatility than stability.

Larger ramifications of a conflict started by killer robots

As killer robots make decisions, there are other, equally important ramifications to think about.

One of the biggest ramifications is that the foreign policy of nations will no longer be driven just by humans. In the age of killer robots, a nation's foreign policy will also be defined by what robots do. Are governments prepared for this?

In September 2013, the US Air Force test fired a new anti-ship missile. Once the missile entered a certain area, communications with it were severed. The missile was flying solo. There were three target ships at sea, and the missile had to decide, autonomously, which of the three ships to attack. The missile ended up attacking a 260-foot ship. The test was to examine how well the missile can function without human input. The missile is being designed to fly over wide areas and decide, on its own, which ships are enemies or friendlies.[4]

Consider what this means. For years, missiles have been considered one of the most powerful weapons a nation can have. The more advanced the missile, such as intercontinental ballistic or hypersonic, the longer the reach of a nation. Except, missiles, like tanks or fighter jets, have always been controlled by humans. Even when they are launched, they are always given a target - by humans. Now, missiles are gaining the ability to pick targets on their own.

These new "AI-missiles" - missiles that use AI to decide on a target on their own - may create new risks for the world.

One of the regions where the US may deploy its AI-missiles may be the Indian Ocean, a region that is becoming increasingly strategic to global trade. The US may be worried about a possible conflict in the Indian Ocean, disrupting global trade, and may deploy its AI-missiles to deter countries from taking aggressive steps. Except, as the US deploys AI-missiles, it will not just be reorienting its military capabilities, but also its foreign policy.

Imagine a conflict taking place between different piracy groups in the Indian Ocean. The piracy groups are from Somalia and Djibouti. To protect its interests and that of its allies, the US dispatches warships that have the AI-missiles. Once the US warships arrive, the conflict intensifies to a point where the US warships launch AI-missiles to protect themselves - and their allies.

Except, also in the area are warships from Vietnam and Thailand. And, the AI missiles accidentally identify those warships also as the enemy and attack them. Many warships coming from regional powers in Southeast Asia are destroyed. The moment this happens, past and present US foreign policy towards Vietnam and Thailand goes out the window. Now, the West and East face a new reality. Since Vietnam and Thailand are members of the Association of Southeast Asian Nations (ASEAN), the entire region condemns the US, and retaliates through economic and political means. The US businesses are banned throughout ASEAN. Then ASEAN halts all exports to the US. The US diplomats are arrested as Vietnam and Thailand demand an apology and compensation from the US. The US refuses. The US introduces new geopolitical variables of its own. What started as a conflict between two piracy groups becomes a totally different geopolitical nightmare. Overnight, decades of diplomacy, trade and relations get destroyed because of the decisions AI-missiles made.

This is another example of how countries might play catch up to what their killer robots have done. In this case, playing catch up means understanding the foreign policy implications of what a killer robot has done.

Another ramification is that a conflict started by killer robots could affect the interests of other nations.

For example, Russia is working on a project called "Project Iceberg." This project calls for fully-autonomous submarines for energy extraction in the Arctic. Belgorod, a Russian nuclear submarine, which is the largest in the world, could be used as a moving base for smaller submarines to dock into. Project Iceberg also calls for "underwater power stations" that will function autonomously and allow submarines to charge.[5]

For now, this project is focused on energy extraction, not defense. But, because of the amount of resources in the Arctic, and the need for nations to protect their territory in the region, nations may militarize their robots.

This would mean that, in the case of Russia, if a situation arises where its submarine's survival is threatened, or where resources considered "Russian" are being stolen, the submarines could take steps to defend themselves.

Also in the Arctic may be killer robots from other nations like China, the US, India and Denmark. Armed robots, from several nations, operating in close proximity to each other could be a recipe for disaster. The robots may perceive situations and think in ways that humans may not.

Eventually, there could be a situation where robots from Denmark are close to "infringing" on Russia's territory in the Arctic. Russia's armed submarines may decide to fire at the Danish robots to warn them to stay away. But, the Danish robots may view this as an attack on them. And, they may fire back at the Russian submarines.

Within minutes, there could be a skirmish in the Arctic between Russia and Denmark, because of killer robots. Just like in the case between Israel and Iran (explored earlier), Russia and Denmark will have to decide whether they support or disavow what their robots have done.

Except, in this situation, there may be other nations involved.

What happens if the skirmish between Russia and Denmark destroys energy deposits "claimed" by the US or China? Or, if several trade vessels owned by Japanese and South Korean companies are damaged? Suddenly, the Russia-Denmark conflict starts to rope in other countries. Now, Russia and Denmark may also have to explain themselves to third-party countries. Or, killer robots from those other countries may retaliate on their own, adding to the conflict. Put simply, what killer robots do may initially involve just one or two countries (i.e. Israel and Iran or Denmark and Russia). But, depending on where the killer robots are, and if other countries are also present, a conflict started by killer robots could fast involve several countries. All of this may happen at such lightening fast speeds, meaning that while killer robots from several countries are attacking each other in the Arctic, governments around the world may learn later what their killer robots have done and why.

Lastly, killer robots could result in a loss of power for certain countries. These countries are the traditional geopolitical powers of the world. And, they draw their power, in part, from "guiding" world affairs.

For example, the US has guided Middle Eastern affairs for decades. If a country makes a major decision in the Middle East, most of the time, the US is in the loop. But, if Israeli autonomous drones attack Iran, starting the next war in the region, the US will be as caught off guard as everyone else. Will the US be perceived as less capable in guiding the Middle East? Will nations think twice about whether the US can actually enforce its will in the age of killer robots? Similarly, if US AI-missiles attack warships in the Indian Ocean, surprising the world, what will this say about Japan, India and China, and the kind of "control" and "influence" they have over Asian affairs?

Because killer robots will have a "mind of their own," their actions may come as a surprise and shock countries everywhere. When this happens, governments may start to view the world as less stable and predictable. And, slowly, governments may lose faith in countries, like the US or Russia, who have traditionally controlled and guided entire regions of the world. If these countries are caught off guard by killer robots, then do they truly control geopolitics?

Conclusion

For nations deploying killer robots, the biggest question is how they will respond once their robots make a decision. Whether the killer robots attack another country, enter another nation without permission or kill innocent civilians during a mission, it will be up to governments to decide what their position is. Do they support the killer robots? Or, do they disavow what the killer robots have done?

It is not just governments who will be forced to pick a side.

Also at risk are firms building the killer robots. After all, governments will be acquiring killer robots from private companies.

Are the firms manufacturing killer robots ready to be blamed if their killer robot "malfunctions" or makes a "bad decision"? Could governments blame a future conflict on the faulty programming of a firm? In turn, large firms might push the blame onto contractors or suppliers.

Even laws may have to change. If a killer robot makes a bad decision, could employees that built the robot face jail time?

The emergence of killer robots also means that manufacturing firms will be partly influencing the foreign policy of nations. This is because the way in which a killer robot is built and programmed, will define the decisions the robot makes. In the past, companies may have manufactured tanks or fighter jets based on the current foreign policy of a nation (the buyer). This was the human-led era. But now, in the age of killer robots, companies will be manufacturing tanks and fighter jets based on a foreign policy that is fluid and unpredictable. In other words, what firms put into their killer robots may influence a nation's foreign policy far more than any diplomatic initiative. This makes the role of private companies far bigger and important than ever before.

This may prompt governments to create new ways to make killer robots accountable for their actions. Governments and militaries may want an "explanation" from killer robots about why they made a certain decision. What data points did they look at? What was their analysis? Was there any bias? To answer these questions, perhaps, companies may be forced to install "autonomous black box" devices in killer robots that record everything the robot is doing.

These boxes would go beyond what currently exists, which track the direction a drone is going, or what pilots are saying in an airplane. Instead, the autonomous black boxes would look at how AI is thinking and the kind of data it has access to. This way, if a killer robot does make a bad decision, there is some record of what happened.

As nations think about deploying killer robots, they may view them as the "end of the road" - the last defensive measure they need to have. They may view killer robots as a deterrence mechanism to stop future wars. But, quite to the contrary, killer robots are actually the beginning of a brand new road. They are the beginning of a new kind of warfare, in which a single decision can snowball and evolve into something nobody imagined.

In that world, killer robots will jolt countries and companies alike. For the first time, heads of state will be awakened at night, executives will be alerted and diplomats will scratch their heads, not over the actions of another human being, but because of the actions of a killer robot (or robots) operating miles away and making decisions on their own. And, forcing countries and companies to explain their actions.

Chapter Two - Controlling The Storm

Creating ethics to influence how killer robots behave

Caracas, Venezuela
2031

In 2031, Venezuela, Russia and China sign a new agreement. This agreement gives Venezuela access to the latest biotechnology advancements from Russia and China. In exchange, Russia and China get the exclusive rights to sell Venezuela their artificial intelligence (AI).

Over the next two years, Venezuela purchases various killer robots from Russia and China.

From Russia, Venezuela buys 25,000 humanoid soldiers and 10,000 autonomous mini-submarines. From China, Venezuela buys 50,000 advanced drones that can rival stealth fighter jets.

Except, as Venezuela buys the killer robots, it faces a conundrum.

One of the conditions that Russia and China set is that Venezuela would use Russian and Chinese ethics in the killer robots. Venezuela agreed to this. But, as Venezuela buys the killer robots, Petrocaribe - formerly an oil alliance and now a diplomatic alliance - steps in. The alliance wants all of its members to use its ethics for killer robots.

Venezuela is divided. Does it use ethics from Russia and China or Petrocaribe?

To appease both parties, Venezuela does something no other country has done before: it programs three sets of ethics into its killer robots. Now, the ethics from Russia and China, along with the ethics from Petrocaribe, are working alongside one another inside the killer robots.

Several governments and businesses warn Venezuela not to do this. They warn that the killer robots could grow unstable and become confused by the different ethics.

As Venezuela deploys its killer robots, it realizes how the three different ethics are clashing with one another. In one instance, Venezuela deploys the killer robots to deal with foreign insurgents that have entered the country and are creating social unrest. Except, the ethics stop the killer robots from killing the insurgents - they only injure them. Why? Because one set of ethics saw the insurgents as "South Americans" entering Venezuela as economic migrants under the trade agreements in place at the time. In another instance, Venezuela deploys the killer robots to assist an ally in the Middle

East to fight a conflict. But, Venezuela's killer robots do not operate at full capacity because they refuse to help the Middle Eastern government. This time a different set of ethics - from China and Russia - were conflicting with the geopolitical agendas of those nations with Venezuela's ally in the Middle East.

Venezuela watches in horror as its killer robots fail to perform. In the end, Venezuela does not blame the killer robots. Instead, it blames the ethics and the countries who are demanding certain ethics be used. As a result, Venezuela starts to rethink its geopolitical relationships. For the first time, ethics, not energy or investment, are defining the relationship between countries.

Introduction

In January 2019, during an event in Washington D.C, a senior official in the US military questioned why people were suggesting that AI should be banned from weapons. He warned that because of the AI capabilities of US adversaries, it may be a mistake for the US not to have AI weapons.[6] His comments reflect the growing feeling when it comes to killer robots. Most governments are thinking about killer robots in terms of defense. But, how do you make a killer robot become an effective defender? This requires making the robots think and behave a certain way.

Except, nations cannot simply deploy an AI-missile defense system or an autonomous submarine and hope that the new autonomous system will do the right thing on its own. The robots must be "programmed" to behave and think in a way that minimizes the risk of mistakes.

One way to influence the behavior of killer robots is through ethics.

This is not a new area considering humans have ethics. For example, most people know that it is not right to randomly attack a stranger on the street. But, does a killer robot understand this? For example, if hundreds of killer robots are deployed by France to protect its embassies throughout Africa, how will these robots know that it is not right to attack civilians? For humans, this is common sense. For killer robots, it might not be.

This is what makes ethics so important. It is ethics that will define the "personality" of killer robots. Without proper ethics, the systems and algorithms governing the robots may have serious issues. The robots may be overly aggressive or perhaps too passive. Also, equally importantly if not more, the killer robots may have more bias towards certain groups of people, affecting how the robots behave with them.

Unlike the deployment of killer robots, which depends on countries, ethics depends on institutions, defense companies and nations. At the same time, the only way to know which ethics are effective, is for killer robots to make decisions. And this means, a killer robot making a mistake, while dangerous, may be the most effective method of knowing which ethics work and which do not.

India turns to ethics to deal with Pakistan

One of the most dangerous hotspots in the world is Kashmir in South Asia.

Since independence, both India and Pakistan have been locked in a long-term conflict. Over the past several decades, they have fought multiple wars. And today, both countries have nuclear weapons.

If a war between India and Pakistan were to take place in the future, it would be devastating, not just for the region, but for the entire world. And yet, even though the risk of a future conflict is high, both countries continue to build capabilities that could take these tensions to new heights.

India, specifically, is investing in advanced military robots. In June 2013, the

Defense Research and Development Organization (DRDO), the Indian military's research and development wing, revealed that they were working on developing "robot soldiers" that would have high intelligence and could determine, autonomously, who is an ally and who is an enemy. One of the areas these robots could be deployed to is the Line of Control (LoC) in Kashmir (the LoC separates the Indian side of Kashmir from the Pakistani side).[7]

For India, the robot soldiers may enhance India's ability to protect and defend its borders. It may also help stop insurgents from entering India. But, as India deploys these robot soldiers, it will not want them to act in ways that could potentially start a conflict with Pakistan. It will want its robot soldiers to have some level of control and understanding.

To enforce this, India may turn to ethics.

For example, several countries are working on ethics for self-driving vehicles. One of them, Germany, has come out with the world's first set of ethics for self-driving vehicles. One of the rules is to ensure that self-driving vehicles do not discriminate towards somebody because of their skin color or gender.

This rule is important because of the decisions self-driving vehicles will be forced to make. If a self-driving vehicle is forced to hit someone in order to stop a more serious accident from taking place, then according to that rule the vehicle is not supposed to hit someone who is darker skinned, or from a specific gender, because of bias in programming.

In the same light, India will also be forced to create ethics that ensure its killer robots behave in a fair and controlled manner with Pakistan. Except, by creating these ethics, India may face an entirely new set of challenges.

Take an ethic called "human life." This ethic would tell a killer robot that human life is extremely precious, and, that before attacking somebody or something, the robot must take every step to avoid conflict.

This is an important ethic, one that most nations would want in their killer robots. Instead of a swarm of autonomous tanks attacking a group of people it suspects are terrorists, this ethic may force the tanks to simply box them in and call for support from human soldiers.

Except, in the coming years, the security challenges India might face could come from robots, not humans. The next time insurgents cross into India from Pakistan, they might be robot soldiers. Does India's "human life" ethic apply to these "robot insurgents"?

Perhaps, it will not. Which means, India will need two sets of ethics. One for humans and another one for robots. While this may seem complicated, it could be fairly simple in the future. Using facial recognition cameras, for example, killer robots could distinguish between a human and robot.

Except, what happens when there is an unmanned tank carrying humans? Now, India's two previous ethics may clash with one another. Or, if India has already predicted this possibility, it could create a third grouping of ethics for robot-human coexistence.

But now, there are three groups of ethics at play in the Indian killer robots. Which will take precedence when? There may be a need for even deeper ethics - a fourth kind - that will drive these three groups of ethics. For example, if human life is on board a robot, does the value of human life change because a robot is involved? In other words, how co-dependent humans and robots are could decide which ethics take priority.

All of this creates an incredibly complicated operating environment. On the one hand, without ethics, killer robots may act in dangerous ways. On the other hand, with ethics, killer robots may be paralyzed or unable to act effectively.

And, India is just one nation. Apply this same complexity to every country, with different security challenges, and the ethics of killer robots becomes a quagmire of confusion and chaos.

There is also the issue of bias that ethics will have to address.

India may take every precaution to ensure its killer robots are not biased towards certain people or countries. And, Indian engineers may do the best they can to program the killer robots to view everyone equally.

Except, one variable has to be taken into consideration: what killer robots learn.

Even if the defense company and military take all precautions to ensure a killer robot does not have any bias, at the end of the day, a bias could simply emerge on its own, based on where and how the killer robot is operating and with what rules of engagement.

For example, if India's killer robots are being constantly deployed in offensive mode to deal with Pakistan and China, but are simultaneously deployed in collaborative mode when working with the US, Russia or Israel, a bias may naturally emerge. The robots may view Pakistan and China with contempt or behave more aggressively. But with the US, Russia or Israel, India's robots may behave very friendly.

On a battlefield, this is incredibly dangerous. If India deploys its biased robots along the LoC, these robots could take risks that India's human soldiers may never take. For example, if Indian and Pakistani forces begin firing at each other alongside the LoC, India's robots might use weapons - like cluster bombs - that human soldiers may never have used in the past. Or, if India's robots identify Chinese soldiers nearing India's borders, the Indian robots might cause physical injury to stop them. Again, this would be a course of action human soldiers may have never taken.

Will this force India, and other countries, to constantly analyze the code in killer robots to identify signs of bias? What if some countries want bias in their robots to make them more effective towards certain nations? Furthermore, what if killer robots reach a point of intelligence where they learn to hide their bias so they are not "reset" or "reprogrammed"?

Whose ethics will nations use for their killer robots?

It is not just countries that will play a big role in developing ethics for killer robots. Equally importantly, global institutions will also have a huge influence on what ethics the world adopts. But, this creates a new challenge for countries. Which institution (or institutions) should they follow?

In the 20th century, this challenge did not exist as there were only a handful of institutions, most of which came from the West. Now, things are different. Alongside the North Atlantic Treaty Organization (NATO), is the Shanghai Cooperation Organization (SCO). Alongside the International Monetary Fund (IMF) and World Bank is the New Development Bank (NDB). Alongside the European Union (EU) is the Association of Southeast Asian Nations (ASEAN). What this means is that different institutions and organizations may set out different ethics and this will put countries in a position that they have not been in before.

Take China, for example. In July, 2018, the Chinese government unveiled a new plan to grow its military power globally. In the 2020s, China wants autonomous submarines in oceans around the world. These submarines will use AI to operate entirely on their own and will be capable of everything from spying to launching "suicide attacks" on enemy ships.[8] As China works on ambitious projects like this, it is very likely that the Chinese military is also working on ethics to govern how its autonomous submarines will behave.

China may want its killer robots to have Chinese ethics. But, what happens if the United

Nations (UN) unveils ethics for killer robots that all member states must use?

This puts China in a troubling situation. Will it reject the UN? Or, will it input the UN ethics as well? Depending on how China plans to use its killer robots, it may or may not accept the UN ethics. And, if China, and several other countries, reject the UN ethics, it will make the UN look weak.

At the same time, China, along with Russia and India, may create their own ethics for killer robots and make them the standard ethics for the entire Shanghai Cooperation Organization (SCO).

But, this puts China, Russia and India, along with the rest of the SCO, in a complex position. Do they follow the UN or SCO? Each institution may have different ethics for killer robots and each institution may have punishments for nations that do not follow their ethics.

This will divide the world. It will also mean that institutions themselves will face a new "relevance challenge." For example, if nations follow SCO over the UN, countries may begin to question the relevance and influence of the UN.

There is also the possibility that nations could group together and create regional or culture-specific ethics for killer robots. For example, the US has been pushing for an "Arab NATO," made up of several countries, in a bid to take on Iran.[9]

If such a group is formed, it would change the Middle East and North Africa. Except, the group might not remain only focused on Iran. It may branch out, and start to dial in on new areas, including killer robots. Could the Middle Eastern nations, through an Arab NATO, propose their own ethics for killer robots? Because most Middle Eastern nations are Islamic, the Arab NATO ethics may stem from Islam too. These ethics might be heavily influenced by Islamic history and teachings. And, because of this, they may differ heavily from the ethics of other defense blocs.

Even without an Arab NATO, the Middle Eastern nations might view ethics for killer robots as an opportunity to join hands, move past historical tensions and maintain their own "unity" and "independence." And that raises the question: could ethics for killer robots bring nations together in new ways or will it divide them even further?

Exporting killer robots with specific ethics

It is one thing to develop ethics and load them into killer robots. It is another thing to export killer robots with specific ethics around the world. This is a new geopolitical opportunity and risk for countries.

For example, in October 2016, Singapore's military announced that it is developing AI to deal with future security challenges. The AI will reduce the number of troops needed but still maintain combat effectiveness. One project revolves around creating "autonomous unmanned systems" that work with human soldiers. Another project revolves around using autonomous systems in place of soldiers for certain missions.[10]

In the coming years, Singapore may take this vision forward by developing certain kinds of killer robots that take the place of humans. But, instead of keeping these killer robots to itself, could Singapore export them to the world?

This may be a geopolitical strategy, by Singapore, to grow its influence in Asia and grow the economy in new ways.

However, as Singapore exports these robots, it will also be exporting Singaporean ethics to other nations. In other words, Singapore may be exporting its culture, beliefs and history to other nations, through killer robots. And, countries buying Singapore's killer robots may not be comfortable with this.

This is an issue that many countries may face. Alongside Singapore, the US, Russia,

China and Israel, will all load their killer robots with unique ethics. Could the "customer countries" mandate that the ethics be changed if they buy them?

Today, a similar issue exists around defense purchases. Many nations around the world are telling defense companies that in exchange for buying their products like fighter jets or tanks or ships, all or some parts of those products must be manufactured in their home countries. In the same light, future nations might tell defense companies or countries, that in exchange for buying killer robots, they must load certain "local ethics" into them or give them options to do it themselves.

The clash of ethics: governments or defense companies?

When it comes to the ethics of killer robots, a major point of contention may be about who should load ethics into killer robots: the government or defense companies making the robots? For most of history, governments have defined the defense strategy and policy of nations. The defense firms made equipment as required by nations. But, in the age of killer robots, some nations may find it more prudent for defense firms to take on the additional role: create ethics. Why? Because defense firms may be seen as having a firmer grasp on robot-driven warfare than governments. After all, it is the defense firms that will be employing AI-engineers and scientists, working alongside former generals and soldiers. Because there will be a huge brain trust in defense firms, they may be far more knowledgeable about what kind of ethics to install.

An example of a company who could create ethics is a Russian missile defense firm, which in July 2017, announced it was working on AI-missiles for the Russian military. These missiles will be able to "think" on their own and allow commanders to redirect the missiles, even add more tasks once the missiles are launched.

In this case, will the Russian government create ethics, and direct the Russian firm to use them? Or, will the Russian firm create the ethics independently?

If the Russian government creates the ethics, it means that Moscow wants to control exactly how its killer robots function. But, if the Russian firm creates the ethics, then it means Moscow is open to allowing its killer robots to behave differently based on who is manufacturing them.

Obviously, there are risks to both approaches. Perhaps, the best way forward is for governments to create underlying, standardized ethics that act as a foundation for killer robots. Then, defense firms can add on to them.

Conclusion

Most research into killer robots has to do with their military capabilities and effectiveness. How effective will an autonomous submarine be compared to current submarines? How much cheaper will autonomous drones be than fighter jets?

These are important questions that need to be answered in order to justify the development or acquisition of killer robots. But, they are not the only areas that the governments and defense companies have to think about when it comes to killer robots.

Ethics for killer robots is as important as the actual development of killer robots. Should a killer robot value life the same way a human does? Is there baseline ethics that every military should hardwire into their killer robots? And, what happens if a nation decides to ignore the world and not put ethics, or create their own ethics?

In short, the personality of killer robots is as important as the technology behind killer robots.

And this means, for the first time, it is not just foreign policy experts and generals that need to be "in the loop" when it comes to killer robots. Also required will be new philosophers and futurists, people from disciplines where they are thinking about the future, and deciding what is right and wrong. For the first time, nations will have to think about their military capabilities through the lens of how killer robots might think, not just what humans alone can think.

As the world builds killer robots, a new storm will be created. Without ethics, this storm may tear apart regions and create chaos. But, with ethics, this storm could be tamed, influenced and perhaps, even controlled.

Chapter Three - Defense Exports 5.0

Regulating the trade around killer robots

Accra, Ghana
2033

In 2025, the African Union (AU) unveils a new blueprint to grow Africa's power and economy. This blueprint depends entirely on new technologies, such as robotics and artificial intelligence (AI).

Over the next several years, this blueprint redesigns the economies of Africa. All kinds of countries become hubs for different areas, such as Ethiopia (deep learning) and Guinea (consumer drones).

But one country, in particular, finds a niche in killer robots: Ghana. By investing in killer robots, Ghana becomes a global hub for providing "brains" of killer robots. Hundreds of startups in Accra, Kumasi and other cities in Ghana, supply the minds of killer robots that are manufactured around the world.

As the Ghanaian startups expand, Ghana runs into an unexpected trouble.

In 2033, dozens of Ghanaian startups expand into Germany, to use it as a hub for their

European operations. Except, the German government bans these startups over killer robot concerns.

For the first time, technology companies are driving defense exports. And, this has put these technology companies in the crosshairs of countries, like Germany, who are against killer robots.

Because of Germany's decision, Ghana and Germany are on a collision course.

In response, Ghana threatens to shut down the "brains" of all killer robots used by the North Atlantic Treaty Organization (NATO), the defensive bloc that Germany is a part of. This jolts the US, the United Kingdom, France and other NATO members, who need the killer robots to function.

These countries pressure Germany to repeal its ban. Within days, Germany complies and changes its position on the ban.

As Ghana's startups are free to operate in Germany, a new reality sets in for the world. A new set of nations, who have built a domestic industry for killer robots, now call the shots. Except, this domestic industry is not dominated by traditional defense firms. It is dominated by a new generation of technology companies that are offering deep specialization in different areas of killer robots.

Introduction

In January 2018, India and Japan announced that they would be working together to jointly-develop AI and robotics for defense. One of the first projects they will work on is creating an unmanned ground vehicle (UGV).[11]

This kind of work, by countries, in the field of military robotics, is a sign of what is to come in the age of killer robots. Nations will work together to jointly develop killer robots. And, this could lead to killer robots rapidly proliferating around the world.

In August 2018, a Russian robotics company said they may export their flagship robot to Uzbekistan by 2020 to work as a police officer. At the time, Kazakhstan had already begun to use the Russian robots. In other words, Russia is exporting police to other nations.[12] While the robots Russia is exporting cannot attack autonomously, the point is that the export of robots that *could* eventually become killer robots has already begun.

When it comes to exporting killer robots, some nations may be hesitant to do so. But this hesitation may disappear for two reasons. First, killer robots could be a lucrative business and a new growth sector for the economy. Second, if certain nations are exporting killer robots, it may push other countries, who may have initially refused, to do the same. For example, if China, Russia and India are exporting killer robots, France and the UK may be forced to also offer their own robots so they do not lose influence. And, so that their allies and partners do not buy military equipment from their competitors.

However, the trade of killer robots is not clear cut. Because of what killer robots mean for the world, the trade of these new "weapons of war" could lead to new challenges and transformations.

Are technology companies the new defense companies?

One of the biggest transformations could be in defining who the *next* defense companies are. In the old world of military trade, which revolved around tanks or missile defense systems, it was the traditional defense firms. But in the world of killer robots, it may be the new and unconventional companies, such as technology companies, driving trade.

Many technology companies are already supplying governments with technologies that underpin killer robots or autonomous systems.

For example, in June 2018, a major US technology company, which specializes in online search, announced it will be ending

"Project Maven" with the Pentagon.[13] The move was triggered by huge backlash from employees of the search company, who felt the work that they were doing was not being used in the right way.

The project, however, sheds light on just how "interlinked" the technology and defense industry is becoming. The project involved using AI to identify people and objects in a drone footage.

In other words, the US technology firm was supplying AI that could help military drones identify future targets. And, even though one US technology firm bowed out of the project, it did not stop other US technology firms from continuing their work with the Pentagon. One of the largest cloud service providers unveiled a new cloud-computing service designed specifically for the intelligence community in November 2017.[14]

These developments point to how the defense world is slowly becoming reliant on technology companies. In the coming years, instead of just supplying technologies, could these technology companies also supply the whole killer robot?

If this happens, things will become blurry, as technology companies morph into defense companies (and if defense companies build killer robots on their own, then defense companies morph into technology companies).

More than anything else, this transformation will mean technology companies could be driving the trade of killer robots. And that means, if governments target killer robot trade, they may be targeting technology firms.

This could create a new clash between countries and technology companies.

Today, when technology companies expand overseas, their investment is welcomed, like in June 2018, when a US technology company announced a new AI-lab in Accra, Ghana. It will be the company's first AI-lab in Africa.[15] Immediately, it set up Ghana as a leading AI-power in Africa. Or, in September 2017, when a separate US e-commerce company announced it was going to open up a second headquarters, cities all over North America submitted their application.[16] If they won the bid, it would change their economy.[17]

But, this may all change when technology companies are building killer robots. Their expansion and global footprint may be viewed negatively.

Tomorrow, if a South Korean technology firm announces a new robotics lab in Chile that will focus on killer robots, the Chilean government may block the bid. Why? Because, Chile may have ruled that killer robots are illegal. And, it may believe that the South Korean company will give "Made in Chile" killer robots to nations that Chile does not approve of. Or, tomorrow, if the African Union (AU) rules against killer robots, then labs, such as the AI-lab in Ghana, may come under scrutiny as they may be seen as supporting the development of killer robots.

At the same time, variables that may not have been on the mind's of defense firms may suddenly create challenges. For example, tomorrow, Switzerland may ban killer robots. And, the Swiss government may create a task force to ensure that all defense and technology firms comply with its ruling. Except, an AI-firm from New Zealand, that sells code for killer robots, may be using Switzerland to store data. Will Switzerland view this as breaking its laws? Will it view data stored in its borders as crossing the line? Are defense and technology firms thinking about these issues? In the age of killer robots, every variable, from sourcing physical parts to buying the brains to storing the data, may become new flash points between companies and countries.

A new paradigm is emerging. In the past, governments had the power to make companies do what they wanted. Going forward, it might be the opposite. That is because, slowly, technology companies are supplying services that entire nations will become dependent on. For example, look at Kuala Lumpur. In January 2018, Kuala Lumpur announced that it was buying an AI-system from a Chinese technology company to make Kuala Lumpur a smart city.[18] This AI will, initially, be helping Kuala Lumpur with transportation. But soon, it could also help in all kinds of areas, from healthcare to policing.

In the future, what if most of Malaysia becomes dependent on AI from Chinese technology firms? If so, it changes the balance of power.

All of a sudden, the Chinese technology companies are in the power position, not the Malaysian government. Then, if a Chinese firm builds an AI-lab in Malaysia to create code for killer robots, there may be little the Malaysian government can do. Even if the Malaysian laws make killer robots illegal, Malaysia may be too dependent on Chinese technology to do anything. Will Malaysia take on Chinese technology companies, and risk losing access to services the various sectors of the country need to survive? In other words, there may be two kinds of companies developing killer robots. The first will build killer robots, export them and perhaps, clash with governments. The second will build killer robots, export them, and continue about their business. This second group of companies will be those that supply other technologies to companies and countries, and who are so powerful, few are willing to take them on or upset them. Because of their power, they could develop killer robots and sell them, with little to no restriction. You can see early signs of this in how many large technology firms are dealing with data, privacy and country laws.

Alongside all of this is the risk of dragging governments into tensions that start because of a company. In January 2019, a US social media company announced a $7.5 million investment in Germany to create a new ethics institute.[19] The institute will help create ethics to govern how AI behaves. Tomorrow, if Germany bans killer robots, will it target this AI-institute? Germany may target the institute because the company behind it may be developing or supplying killer robots or code. This puts a US firm in the crosshairs of the German government. If the German government raids the AI-institute and shuts it down, it may anger the US government. What will the US do if one of its most valuable technology companies has been targeted by Germany because of killer robots? Such a move is likely to affect US-Germany relations.

Because technology firms will be supplying services that power economies and societies, they may have "carte blanche."

Technology companies could do whatever they want and get away with it, including developing and selling killer robots. All of this translates into a new era beginning for technology companies and governments. But it also means, because technology companies will have little restriction, they could sell killer robots on a huge scale. And, they could do so with a speed that takes "autonomous weapons" around the world faster than anyone expected.

New trade rules around exporting/importing killer robots

The biggest challenge around the trade of killer robots is how nations and institutions may seek to control and regulate this trade.

For example, today, there exists an organization called the "Nuclear Suppliers Group (NSG)," which regulates and stops the proliferation of nuclear weapons and related technology. Dozens of nations belong to NSG. The membership grants nations access to a variety of highly-restricted technologies. This is one of the reasons why India has been trying to join the NSG, as joining it would give India access to more plutonium, which in turn, India can use for its thorium program (a program designed to enhance India's energy independence and reduce greenhouse gases).[20]

In the same light, the world may create a new group for killer robots, such as the "Robot Suppliers Group" (RSG), which controls and regulates killer robots, and technologies related to them.

But, unlike the NSG, which was created in the 20th century when the world was largely unipolar, the RSG would be created at a time when the world is more multipolar. Who has the right to create RSG? And, who has the right to deny another country access to RSG?

The US, for example, may prefer to create an RSG with select countries, such as UK, France, Germany, Israel, Japan, South Korea and India. This may prompt other world powers, like Russia and China, to create their own RSG, and include other nations, like UAE, Iran and Venezuela.

And this means that all of a sudden, there will be two or more regulatory organizations for killer robots. Will these organizations effectively cancel each other out? How will these organizations coexist with one another? Which RSG will the rest of the world follow?

Consider what this means for killer robots.

If most countries in Asia join the RSG led by China and Russia, it means that most of Asia is conforming to rules and requirements that the Asian RSG is setting. And, the Chinese and Russian RSG may give countries access to technology that the US RSG does not.

In a future conflict in Asia, killer robots from countries that are part of the US RSG, may have less capabilities than killer robots from countries that are part of the Asian RSG. How will this affect the conflict? Will some countries killer robots be destroyed more easily?

There is also the role that global institutions and trade blocs, like the World Trade Organization (WTO), the European Union (EU), the Association of Southeast Asian Nations (ASEAN) and the Eurasian Economic Union (EEU) will play in regulating the trade of killer robots.

These institutions and trade blocs will have to define how killer robots can be traded between member states. And, if member states are not happy with their institution or trade bloc, they may jump to another, or create their own. But, what kind of rules might these different groups implement?

In July 2017, a leading Russian defense firm announced that it is developing autonomous combat drones that use AI to decide what to do in different situations. The drones will use AI to decide which person is a target and how best to respond.[21] The Russian firm is also behind a combat robot tank that has autonomous capabilities.[22]

Should the Russian firm successfully develop these drones, it will provide Russia with a brand new source of revenue. And, the Russian firm, after getting approval from the Russian government, may decide to export these drones to members of the EEU, a trade bloc which Russia leads.

This could be a geopolitical play, by Russia, to ensure that members of the EEU stay within Russia's orbit and do not move to China's or America's. However, will Russia simply export these drones, the same way it may have exported previous defense exports? Or, will Russia take a different route?

For example, Russia may mandate that EEU members who want access to Russian killer robots must connect these robots to a central Russian "brain." The thinking and personality of killer robots operating in Kazakhstan, Uzbekistan and other EEU member states would be rooted in servers in Moscow or St. Petersburg.

In other words, Russia will be effectively controlling the military capabilities of other nations. And, while at first glance, this may seem unacceptable, countries might actually accept this condition. Why? Because, while nations may be wary over giving Russia this kind of control over their robot military capabilities, they may overlook this concern since they are getting access to weapons that could change their military capabilities and readiness.

Alternatively, Russia may chart an entirely brand new course for itself. It might create a new "app ecosystem" for killer robots. And, it might invite EEU members to build apps. For example, an engineer might build an app for autonomous submarine that allows it to monitor sea creatures for any gene editing - a sign that governments may have played with part of the environment. This could be a new industry for EEU members, allowing engineers, executives and ethicists to build apps they feel are important. This in turn will give defense firms the ability to install new capabilities, or offer new features built by a "third party community." By utilizing its trade bloc, Russia could set itself apart from everyone else, and bring countries deeper into its orbit in a brand new way.

Because of killer robots, how nations trade with each other could change. Not only might new trade blocs emerge, shifting geopolitical power, but existing trade blocs could be reconfigured to revolve around killer robots. The age of killer robots then, is not just about bringing new weapons to the world. It is also about changing how countries are connected to one another.

Controlling dual-use technologies around killer robots

As with any revolutionary technology, there could be international moratoriums on killer robots. Or, some nations, and the international community, may view killer robots as so dangerous to humanity, that they may outright ban them.

Except, regardless of what laws the world passes to try and stop killer robots from being developed and deployed, many countries may secretly develop them.

All of this leads to the issue of dual-use technologies.

These are technologies that nations export for one reason, but can be used for another. The issue of dual-use technologies has long been attached to North Korea and China, as some nations, especially in the West, feel that China has exported technology to Pyongyang that appears to be civilian in nature, but has military applications.

Similarly, considering the parts and materials that make killer robots could also be used to build industrial robots, consumer drones or self-driving buses, the world may have a hard time controlling what materials nations are exporting, and how these materials could be used to build killer robots.

For example, in the future, there may be concerns that countries in Europe are building killer robots for dangerous reasons. To stop these countries, the international community may try to block certain materials from entering Europe. But, if 95% of materials used to build killer robots are also being used to build regular robots, what will the international community do?

If the world cannot outright block the trade of certain materials, then they may turn to other routes. For example, could they start tracking materials in a new way?

In July 2018, a leading US technology services company unveiled a new solution to enforce intellectual property (IP) ownership of algorithms. The company wants to add a "watermark" to the basic code of an algorithm.[23] That way if the algorithm is stolen or sold without permission, people can analyze the code and see the watermark (the original owner). Could there be a similar solution to track certain materials and be alerted when they are being used to build killer robots? Perhaps, the world could also set up a blockchain-based trading system, which monitors global trade in real time. Then, the international community can track how much of a certain material is entering specific nations.

Of course, this assumes that nations will be comfortable allowing their imports and exports to be monitored. However, if there is no system in place to track the technologies/materials used to build killer robots, then nations may be free to build them, without limits.

There's also the issue of certain people and groups freely providing the technical guides on how to build killer robots. This could be in the form of videos online or manuals spread through torrent websites. This does not necessarily have to be a video titled, "How To Build An Autonomous Drone Armed With Weapons." Instead, it could be a video titled, "How To Bring Self-Driving Capabilities To Your Vehicle For Under $200." By bringing self-driving capabilities to a normal vehicle, regular vehicles may be used as new weapons. Certain groups might learn to develop their own self-driving cars to create chaos in society, like running over people on a sidewalk or crashing into malls.

Again, because the materials and parts used to build killer robots may be mainstream and accessible everywhere, the know-how on how to build killer robots may also be freely available. Governments and intelligence agencies must prepare for this.

Equally important is that "online" does not just mean Internet forums or videos anymore. It could also mean virtual reality worlds, where people can build killer robots from the ground up, and teach others how to do the same thing. And, in the age of additive manufacturing (3D printing), certain parts may be printed at home, not purchased anywhere - creating new challenges around tracking materials and parts.

Also, consider that buying killer robots may clash with constitutional rights. For example, in the US, the second amendment allows people to bear arms. People can buy guns in the US in ways that are not possible in other parts of the world. But, will the US government allow people to buy killer robots? If somebody can purchase a semi-automatic rifle, should they also be allowed to purchase armed drones? Perhaps, people may want such drones for home security.

If governments do not think about these issues today, then people may act out of their own judgement. And, this could create the next constitutional crises, as people interpret the constitution differently from the government.

Who maintains control of the robots once they are sold?

The issues around the trade of killer robots do not end once the killer robots themselves are exported/imported. Once the killer robots are sold, and are deployed by a particular nation, there will be challenges around just how much control the "buyer" nation has over their new weapons.

For example, in December 2017, it was revealed that the F-35 fighter jets that Norway purchased from the US were sending "sensitive data" back to the US. This data allowed the manufacturer of the fighter jets to monitor the behavior and decisions of Norwegian pilots.[24]

Such issues will be magnified in the age of killer robots.

In December 2016, a group in China tested a swarm of 67 drones flying together. The drones were able to communicate with one another in order to carry out reconnaissance, intelligence and surveillance objectives.[25] The Chinese swarm beat the record held by the US (50 drones acting as a swarm).

Importantly, unlike the US drones which were launched from "modern" launchers, the Chinese drones were launched from rubber bands, allowing China to launch faster in a future conflict. At the same time, in a video recorded to show the Chinese drone swarm, was a clip of how the drone swarm could be used for a "saturation attack" (multiple drones attacking a single target).[26]

In the coming years, once China refines this technology, it may decide to export it. One country that may purchase it is Mexico. The Mexican government may want this technology to help crack down on drug smuggling. And, Mexico may purchase this technology from China, on purpose, to send a message to the US that it could change its geopolitical orientation, through technology.

But once Mexico gets its hands on this technology, will Mexico be in control or China?

While 90% of the time, Mexico may be in control of the drones, there may be instances when China could take over. And, these few instances, where China takes control, may strike fear in the US. If there is a future conflict between the US and China, the drones in Mexico may pose a national security risk to the US. What will the US do to deter Mexico from buying or using the Chinese drones? And, how will China prove that it has no backdoor?

There is also the question of data and cyber security.

In the old world of military trade, data and cybersecurity were not as important. But, today, in the age of killer robots, it is extremely important. After all, the data from killer robots may provide deep insight into battlefields, foreign lands and the military strategies of nations. And, cyber security, or lack of, could determine whether killer robots are a military strength or vulnerability.

In the case of Mexico, the Mexican government may force the Chinese drones to store data within Mexico. But the moment that happens, it may invoke data laws around the United States Mexico Canada Agreement (USMCA), which require data to be stored in the US (in certain cases).

At the same time, how will Mexico ensure its cyber security is up to acceptable standards (standards that Mexico may not have had a say in setting)? Mexico could "trust" the Chinese manufacturer. Or, Mexico might force the Chinese manufacturer to integrate cyber security that Mexico wants. And this could complicate matters if the cyber security that Mexico wants comes from the US. China may not want cyber security from the US protecting its drones, as this cyber security may also have access to the entire drone and its systems, giving the US insight into the Chinese weapons.

These issues highlight other, more indirect ways in which killer robots could create new challenges as they are traded and sold around the world.

Conclusion

As nations look to killer robots to enhance their power and maintain their control over certain regions of the world, the assumption is that killer robots will be allowed to be developed and deployed in the first place.

What if these robots are banned from the get-go? Or, what if only a handful of countries have them and refuse to export them to the rest of the world? This would mean that large swaths of the world may be without the new military capabilities that could change the balance of power in the world.

Ultimately, the trade of killer robots is about control. It is about ensuring that killer robots do not proliferate around the world, unfettered, or reach the hands of every and any military (or rogue group).

But, as nations seek to enforce their will, they will struggle to find the right balance and to ensure that other nations follow their way and not someone else's. At the same time, major headaches will emerge as to how to stop nations from building killer robots, considering the parts and materials may be freely available.

Perhaps, to control killer robots, nations will turn to controlling the AI.

After all, nations may be able to build the physical structure of an autonomous tank or drone, but the "brains" may be the hardest part to acquire. This could lead to a group called the "AI Suppliers Group," or AISG, to control algorithms and systems used in killer robots. But, even here, challenges emerge, such as to how to stop experts from recreating the "minds" of killer robots and selling them on the black market.

All of this leads to the real possibility that nations will have to prepare for a loss of control and vacuum of leadership when it comes to killer robots.

No trade policy or organization will be able to fully stop the spread of killer robots. New trade rules and paradigms may emerge that not only influence how killer robots move between countries but also how nations grow their power.

For the past several decades, the term "military industrial complex" has been used to describe the power and influence that defense companies have. But, this term may be in need of updating. Perhaps, in the age of killer robots, the new term should "robotics industrial complex" as robotics companies, and technology companies, drive the development, and trade, of weapons that every nation will want.

Chapter Four - Preparing For The Unexpected

Future possibilities that could emerge from killer robots

Tallinn, Estonia
2035

In 2027, Estonia leads the creation of a new consortium in Eastern and Central Europe called "Security Through Autonomous Robots" or STAR. This new consortium, made up of several countries in the region, will focus on manufacturing killer robots and offering them as mercenaries to foreign governments and organizations.

By 2033, STAR has hundreds of thousands of killer robots operating around the world as mercenaries. From Latin America to Southeast Asia, STAR is offering governments and other groups, military capabilities they never had access to before.

In 2035, a civil war takes place in Argentina. And, STAR is caught in the middle of it.

A political faction in Argentina breaks off from the government and stages a coup. And, to enforce its will, it uses robot mercenaries it quietly purchased from STAR several months earlier. The political faction surrounds the house of the Argentinian head of state with autonomous tanks and rounds up members of government with humanoid robots.

Following this, opposing groups begin fighting on the streets. One side wants the political faction that staged the coup to give back control. The other side supports the political faction and wants to see the former government toppled.

As the world watches what is taking place, several governments begin to blame STAR.

They say that the only reason the political faction in Argentina was able to stage a coup was because it had access to robot mercenaries. If these robot mercenaries did not exist, it would have been impossible to stage a coup and do what they did so effectively.

STAR refuses to accept this. STAR's leadership, in Tallinn, puts out a statement that says it will sell robot mercenaries to anyone it wishes, and that just because someone uses the mercenaries a certain way, does not make STAR accountable for their actions.

But, behind closed doors, STAR is worried. It knows that its robot mercenaries are partly responsible for the civil war in Argentina. But, more than anything else, STAR is worried because at least 17 other political factions around the world have purchased killer robot mercenaries as well.

And, the deliveries will begin within the next few weeks.

STAR braces itself for more political instability around the world. And, the blame that is likely to follow.

Introduction

So far, killer robots have been looked at solely from the defense perspective, like, how will killer robots affect warfare? Or, could killer robots start wars?

Except, this is not the whole picture. Because killer robots represent a brand new capability that has never existed before, killer robots could be used in ways nobody has expected or imagined. Just as nobody predicted the Internet would give rise cyber attacks, or that artificial intelligence (AI) would bring about a new "deepfakes" challenge, so too, there is no telling how killer robots might be used and applied beyond the government control.

Could countries "hire" killer robots?

In March 2019, the Advanced Research Foundation, the research and development wing of the Russian military, unveiled new ground-based robot soldiers. These soldiers are essentially tanks that can operate alongside human assets on a battlefield. According to the research foundation, it wants to eventually give these robots the ability to select targets and control the weapons systems - something humans are in control of right now.[27]

What the Russian military robots represent are the next soldiers for militaries around the world. In future conflicts, militaries may deploy thousands of these autonomous tanks instead of human soldiers.

As this kind of technology is refined, a new possibility emerges. Could these killer robots serve as the next mercenaries?

Today, there are dozens of organizations offering mercenary services. One of the most famous has a 7,000 acre compound in North Carolina, where it trains the recruits. And, its mercenary army is over 20,000.[28] In fact, in January 2019, following the US announcement that it would be pulling troops from Syria, the former head of the mercenary group proposed sending in mercenaries to replace the soldiers that were going to leave.[29]

Except, until now, mercenaries have always been humans. But, if killer robots become mercenaries, it changes the rules.

For one, killer robots as mercenaries means that any company could supply mercenaries in the coming years. As long as they have the resources to buy the robots, companies of all shapes and sizes could offer mercenary services to governments globally. Not only will this create competition for existing mercenary companies, but it will also create a new supply of soldiers that governments or groups can tap. Could this result into more geopolitical instability around the world?

For example, if a political faction in a country wants to defect and stage a coup, that faction will need soldiers to enforce its will. In the past, human mercenaries may have been in limited numbers. But, in the age of killer robots, the political faction may have a new option. Could they order 20,000 killer robots to work for them?

There are also serious ethical issues that get raised when killer robots are the mercenaries. Many of these issues already exist, but they will be elevated to new levels with killer robots.

One of the most important questions is: what are killer robots allowed to do?

For example, Somalia has been turning to mercenaries to deal with a piracy problem. Pirates have been hijacking trade vessels and demanding ransom and the Somalian government has struggled to crack down on it.[30]

For now, human mercenaries may be helping. But, in the future, if Somalia wants more military capabilities, could it turn to killer robot mercenaries?

If so, these mercenaries may behave in ways that Somalia or the world does not feel is ethical. What if the robot mercenaries attack pirates in a way that humans would never do, such as decapitating them or blocking their ships and making them starve at sea? Or, what if the robot mercenaries try to sink the vessel they are supposed to protect, because the robots believe they will not be able to protect the vessel from incoming pirates? Or, what happens if pirates bring young children and women on their missions to appear innocent but the robot mercenaries still attack and kill them - including their families?

All of this leads to the question of whether killer robot mercenaries can be held accountable for their behavior.

For example, for many years, India has been dealing with a domestic insurgency problem in the North East. Indian soldiers have died fighting the insurgents and the Indian government has struggled to quell the fighting. In the future, to deal with the insurgents, India may turn to killer robot mercenaries. And, the Indian government might buy 50,000 killer robot mercenaries from a firm in Brazil. These robots may then be stationed throughout India's northeastern corridor as the first line of defense in fighting the insurgents.

Except, what happens if these robot mercenaries start acting out of order, murdering innocent civilians or disrupting trade corridors?

India may be furious if this happens. And, New Delhi will likely blame the Brazilian firm supplying the killer robots. It might hold the Brazilian firm accountable. But, what if the Brazilian firm does not feel the same way and views the conduct of its killer robots as normal, even right? Now this will create a clash between India and the Brazilian firm over the way the killer robots are behaving. And, if the Brazilian firm is state-owned, it puts India and Brazil on a collision course.

Or, perhaps the Brazilian firm will put the blame on the company that programmed the killer robots. This company might be from Japan. Now, both Brazil and India may go after the Japanese firm, which may force the Japanese government to step in. Except, the Japanese firm may then blame contractors it hired, who may be based in France. In the end, who is accountable may never be known as countries and companies play the "blame game."

At the same time, regardless of whether the Brazilian firm takes action or not, India will have social challenges. People in India may be horrified at how the killer robots have behaved and they may start attacking the robot mercenaries. Now, India may have to protect the robot mercenaries from its own people. Or, if the robots are badly damaged, the Brazilian firm may demand reimbursement from the Indian government. Have countries or defense companies thought about this?

Another question to consider is who the next mercenary companies might be.

As mentioned earlier, because killer robots could be easily available, a plethora of new companies could emerge to provide killer robots as mercenaries. This means, it will not just be traditional mercenary companies. It could be a new company, started by a venture capitalist in San Francisco. Or, mercenary services could be a new service that a robotics company in Tokyo offers.

And, since the companies offering mercenary services may change, the places where the next mercenary companies come from may be unexpected. Instead of North Carolina, could it be Bengaluru? Instead of Washington D.C, could it be Silicon Valley? What about Finland or Ethiopia?

These places have never been hubs for mercenary services, but with killer robots, it may simply be a matter of investment and vision. An even more radical possibility is that some governments could create their own mercenary wing and offer killer robot mercenaries to the world. This could be a new way to grow the economy.

Connected to all of these challenges is "desensitization" - that is, not taking the behavior of killer robots seriously because of what is considered "normal."

In February 2018, reports emerged that more than 200 Russian mercenaries were killed in Syria. They were killed in airstrikes by coalition fighter jets.[31] The world held its breath. Would Moscow view the attack as if it were an attack on its own soldiers?

Russia, surprisingly, did not react aggressively. While the world moved on, a new precedent was set, and overlooked: attacking and killing mercenaries is not the same as with uniformed soldiers. In the age of killer robots, will this still be the case?

As killer robots become the next mercenaries, there may be a situation where thousands of killer robots, working as mercenaries, are destroyed. Perhaps, they are destroyed in an electromagnetic pulse (EMP), followed by a large-scale bombing mission. And this may change the balance of power in a conflict so significantly, that the side that destroyed killer robots begins to advance rapidly.

But, will the "killing" of killer robot mercenaries be acceptable?

As the world becomes flooded with killer robot mercenaries, human mercenaries and human soldiers may slowly disappear from the front lines as militaries become "automated." All of this means that governments and groups could become heavily dependent on killer robot mercenaries in all kinds of ways. Losing them could mean losing power over a region, or losing an entire battle. Could the country whose killer robot mercenaries have been destroyed view the attack as an act of war?

Could borders move because of killer robots?

Another new possibility is that killer robots could change the borders of countries. What might this look like?

In May 2016, one of the largest state-owned shipping companies in China unveiled a new plan dubbed the "Underwater Great Wall." The idea is to use advanced sensors and drones, scattered throughout the ocean floor and surface of the South China Sea, to expand China's power in the region.[32] China will know the movements of enemy vessels and may be able to enforce its will much easier. By October 2016, China was in the third phase of deploying the

"Underwater Great Wall,"[33] and in May 2017, China announced $270 million in funding to take the project to the next level.[34]

These drones, which may be armed and fully autonomous in the coming years, could be considered killer robots.

As the world watches China deploy these robots in the South China Sea, little attention is being paid to what the geopolitical implications of this development are.

These robots (and sensors) constitute a new kind of border for China. Wherever the drones go in the South China Sea, they will represent China's borders, the new boundaries of where China begins and ends.

Consider how these drones might operate. At one moment, 2,000 drones may be a few dozen miles north of Indonesia. At another moment, they might be encircling the Philippines. Wherever these drones are, China will be enforcing its will. Ships and vessels will either be able to move freely or they may be restricted. China's borders would be expanding and contracting based on where its drones are.

How will Indonesia or the Philippines react if their trade ships or warships cannot move past a certain point because of the presence of China's killer robots? How will the US conduct the next "Freedom of Navigation (FON)" exercises if China is using its underwater killer robots, guided by sensors, to predict where US warships will be and disrupt their route? Is the US willing to fire on the Chinese drones? And what happens if China's drones are interrupting the movement of armed and autonomous drones belonging to other countries?

There is also the question of just how China's drones will think.

Initially, China's drones may be using the data they are getting from sensors. The Chinese navy and Chinese intelligence agencies may also be supplying data to the drones as well. But, over time, the drones may build their own intelligence and "thoughts" about the South China Sea (or whatever region they are in). And, they may move and spread out on their own, regardless of what the sensors are saying.

And this means, the map of China could change, not because of China's diplomats, but because of China's highly intelligent drones. Is the world ready for this?

Could institutions reinvent themselves through killer robots?

Another possibility is that institutions could reinvent themselves through killer robots.

Many institutions today have a single area of focus. And, they have been operating in these areas for decades now. Even more so, the capabilities that these institutions have, and the structure of these institutions, have not significantly changed over the years.

Take the United Nations (UN).

The UN is largely dependent on how its member states vote, and what the member states provide, from funding to soldiers. And, this limits what the UN can do. If it wants to solve a problem in Bolivia, it needs consent and resources. And, if those do not come, its hands are tied.

In the age of killer robots, this may change. The UN may have a new kind of independence to do what it wants.

For example, instead of depending on member states for soldiers, the UN could instead acquire its own force of killer robots. The UN may have a standing force of 250,000 killer robots. This force may include everything, from humanoid soldiers to autonomous drones to autonomous tanks and AI-cyber soldiers.

This would mean that for the first time since its inception, the UN would be truly independent in what it can do. Because it does not need soldiers from member states, it may be able to make decisions it could not make before. And, because managing killer robots may be significantly cheaper than managing human soldiers, the UN may not need as much funding as before.

Could the UN create a new security zone in a part of Africa even if its member states oppose this? Or, could the UN intervene in a conflict in South America without informing neighboring countries? Of course, governments around the world might restrict access to UN robot soldiers. Or, those same governments could threaten to cut funding if the UN does not stop. But, if the UN can overcome these reactions, it will be able to create an independent foreign policy for itself and deal with global challenges in a brand new way.

This is not just about the UN having independence. This is also about the broader implications of an institution, such as the UN, having its own military. This has not happened in recent history, whereby an institution has its own, independent military, that is not "supplied" by the member states.

How will the "international community" deal with an institution having its own military? Can an institution go to war with a country? For example, if the UN sends in dozens of autonomous warships into the South China Sea to protect certain natural islands and coral reefs from being damaged, what happens if China or the US fires on the UN warships? Or, what happens if the UN's killer robots fire on a Chinese or US vessel?

The idea that an institution, that is bound by traditions and is always dependent on its member states, can act on its own, without depending on its donors, will be a new and different kind of geopolitical paradigm. Because the world has not dealt with institutions having their own independent military, the governments around the world may not have thought of new possibilities and how to deal with them.

There is also the question of how certain institutions can grow and reinvent themselves in the age of killer robots.

Take NATO. Because NATO was created during the Cold War, its main focus has been the Soviet Union, and now the present day Russia. But, with killer robots, could NATO expand out of Europe and carve out a new role for itself?

For example, NATO could purchase 500,000 killer robots. Like with the UN, the NATO robot army may be diverse. And, NATO might deploy 100,000 robots to Africa, as a way to expand beyond Europe. In Africa, NATO might open up fully automated bases, where its robot soldiers provide humanitarian assistance or assist NATO members in military missions. But, these robot soldiers could also be used in a new way. Could NATO program these soldiers to also act as local police forces for governments in Africa? Because it takes time to train police, not to mention control corruption, certain African governments may gravitate towards the robot police officers sourced from NATO. Not only would NATO create a new kind of revenue for itself, it would also provide its members with a new doorway into Africa.

Of course, some NATO members may not be happy. They may view NATO's presence in Africa as a challenge to their own ambitions.

Lastly, killer robots may also allow institutions to imagine a new kind of future for themselves.

For example, for several decades, an organization called the "South Asian Association for Regional Cooperation" (SAARC) has existed. Its mandate, which has changed over the years, is mainly to unite countries in South Asia, through trade and foreign policy. Except, SAARC has not grown in influence to the same extent as the ASEAN Economic Community (AEC), the One Belt, One Road (OBOR) or the Eurasian Economic Union (EEU).

With killer robots though, SAARC could have a new future.

SAARC nations could join hands to launch a new defense institution, fueled in large part by killer robots. Perhaps, India and Pakistan could push forward with this institution as a way to sort out their differences and connect with each other in a brand new way.

As the defense bloc grows, it could have bases in each member state. And, it would mean that South Asian nations have a new kind of independence and geopolitical autonomy. Instead of depending on military support from "external" nations, countries in South Asia, like India, Pakistan, Sri Lanka, Nepal and Bhutan, could depend on their own robotic militaries instead.

Could SAARC expand outward, and also involve countries like Iran or Afghanistan? Because killer robots may be easier and cheaper to acquire than conventional militaries, there is the possibility that certain nations will seize this opportunity and create institutions to expand their own influence.

From South Asia to South America, existing institutions could create a new future for themselves or brand new institutions could emerge, in large part, thanks to killer robots and their military capabilities.

Conclusion

While the world looks at killer robots through the eyes of governments, there are other possibilities that never get mentioned. This includes the creation of brand new robot mercenaries or truly independent institutions.

These new possibilities are major shifts in areas that have remained the same for decades. And, these shifts could bring about immense geopolitical change in the world: from the way in which existing conflict zones evolve to the way in which future challenges are dealt with to the way in which institutions and organizations use killer robots.

In fact, it may not just be institutions like the UN or NATO, or organizations such as mercenary groups, that use killer robots. It might also be businesses.

Consider that killer robots do not just encompass physical machines but also digital robots such as advanced AI systems that can conduct cyber attacks on their own. Could businesses purchase such systems and have in-house cyber divisions that launch attacks at entities (companies or groups) that attack them? Could the next cyber war be between companies, not countries?

All of this is just the tip of the iceberg when it comes to killer robots and the new possibilities they could create for the world. Of course, no possibility is without risks. But, even the risks are likely to do little to deter groups from acquiring and using killer robots. In the end, the big question when it comes to killer robots, is the same one that many governments have asked when acquiring other new technologies: what will I gain? How a nation, institution or company answers this question will define advantage and disadvantage from killer robots.

Chapter Five - Global Fallout
Connecting and controlling the world's killer robots

Astana, Kazakhstan
2037

As a new war begins in Central Asia, Kazakhstan decides to invest in a brand new military. It sets aside $25 billion to purchase huge numbers of killer robots, such as humanoid soldiers, missiles powered by artificial intelligence (AI) and autonomous tanks.

The government does not deploy these assets immediately, but instead, keeps them in reserves. If a situation arises where they are needed, Kazakhstan can activate and deploy them.

After a few months, deadly explosions rock office buildings in Astana. The group behind the explosions warns that Kazakhstan will face more such attacks. The group behind the explosions is the same group driving the war in Central Asia. This pulls Kazakhstan into the conflict. Except, Kazakhstan does not deploy its human military. Instead, it deploys killer robots.

The Kazakh killer robots operate alongside human soldiers and robots from Azerbaijan, Uzbekistan and Kyrgyzstan. But, while the Kazakh killer robots are effective at taking out the enemy, they are also involved in numerous friendly fire incidents that raise tensions between Kazakhstan and several Central Asian nations.

As the war winds down, Kazakhstan recalls its killer robots and starts to analyze what can be done to ensure these friendly fire incidents do not take place in the future. A futurist proposes the idea of a "global brain" that connects all killer robots and updates the robots on the new geopolitical realities, along with the old historical treaties, accords and alliances.

Kazakhstan jumps at this idea.

Over the next six months, Kazakhstan builds this brain. And then, it begins to offer it to other countries. Within one year, Kazakhstan has brought in countries like the US, China, Russia, Japan, India and Israel.

As more countries join, Kazakhstan gains a new kind of geopolitical power. Thanks to the global brain, the world is dependent on Kazakhstan for peace and security in the age of killer robots.

Except, several countries are not happy with the global brain in Kazakhstan. They believe it to be biased and unfair. So, they are quietly building their own brain. And, they plan to use it to compete with Kazakhstan.

Controlling the brains of killer robots is a new kind of competition between nations.

Introduction

In March 2019, the foreign minister of Germany called on the world to take steps to ban "lethal weapons" as a preemptive step towards banning killer robots. The foreign minister made the comments during an arms conference in Berlin, saying, "fundamentally, it's about whether we control the technology or it controls us."[35]

His comments reflect the predicament the world faces. Should the world control killer robots, or will killer robots operate out of control? Except, right now, the only ideas that are being explored, when it comes to controlling killer robots, is banning them. This, unfortunately, is not a realistic solution. Since the major world powers are already developing killer robots, a ban will have little effect on the world.

Instead, countries should look to alternative means to control killer robots. Part of this was explored with ethics that influence the personality of killer robots. But, there are other ways in which the world could control killer robots as well. These ways will require international collaboration and cooperation on a level that may be unimaginable today. But, when the tradeoff is peace over war, perhaps, nations will come together.

Global brains to connect and control killer robots

In February 2016, the US Defense Advanced Research Projects Agency (DARPA) unveiled a new project called "Eyeriss." The project revolves around a new kind of chip that DARPA is developing to allow battlefield robots to think for themselves. The chip is small enough to fit in smartphones but has 168 cores (the average smartphone chip has four cores). Robots that use Eyeriss will be able to do things like informing soldiers that a new threat has been detected.[36]

Like many other projects already explored, Eyeriss reflects the coming autonomy that military robots will have in the future.

To control killer robots, could the world connect all these robots to a "central brain"? What exactly is a central brain? A central brain would be an AI system that houses all of the world's accords, treaties, history and laws. For example, it would house the mutual defense treaty between the US and Japan, and the US and South Korea. These treaties state that if Japan, or South Korea, go to war, or are attacked, the US will protect and defend them. In other words, if a country goes to war with Japan or South Korea, they also go to war with the US.

This central brain could be governed by an international authority. Its duty would be to ensure the brain functions properly and that it is updated based on the changing world situations.

The goal of having a central brain is that every killer robot would be connected to it, and would be on the same page, regardless of which nation the robots are coming from. While this may stop killer robots from making dangerous decisions, it does not come without its own challenges.

One of the biggest challenges may be loyalty. Who is the central brain loyal to?

In the future, if killer robots from China and Japan are facing off in the East China Sea, the central brain may inform them of the ramifications of escalating and attacking one another. But, what if the central brain only informs the Chinese robots, not the Japanese? In this scenario, the central brain would be telling China to back off, but not Japan.

This may horrify China. The Chinese government will question who the central brain is loyal to. Is it loyal to the West? Is it allowing Japan to do whatever it wants while restricting China?

This leads to the next challenge. What does a country do if it finds a problem with the central brain?

For example, in the case of China and Japan facing off, the Chinese government may feel that the central brain has bias towards China. That is why it is always telling China to back off, or move out of the area, not Japan. To deal with China's concerns, perhaps, the authority in charge of the central brain, can offer a transparency report. In other words, if China believes there is a bias, it could access a transparency report to see exactly how the brain is functioning, through every line of code. Of course, this may not be enough to satisfy China's concerns. After all, the report could be manipulated. Therefore, China might also ask for a direct line to the central brain to watch, in real time, what is taking place.

Naturally, there will also be questions about how changes can be made to the central brain.

For example, after the central brain is instituted, Russia and China may create a new accord around fresh water. However, after a while, tensions may rise between Russia and China, and both countries might walk away from the fresh water accord. How does Russia tell the central brain to repeal the accord?

One way may be to have a voting system. Here, members would vote on changes to the central brain. In the case of Russia and China, if more than 50% of members agree with Russia, the fresh water accord can be overturned. But if less than 50% of members agree, the fresh water accord remains intact.

If this is the rule, there may be worries of voter influence. Countries may lobby others to support them so certain agreements or treaties are not removed from the central brain. Or, founding countries of the central brain may have veto power, meaning they could decide whether certain agreements and treaties are ever removed, updated or replaced.

To ensure fairness and objectivity, the institution may push aside ideas like majority votes or vetoes and instead appoint AI to decide what to do. Based on the way AI is predicting events and collating data, it may be able to make decisions about which accords to update or which treaties to repeal better than humans.

There is also the other tasks that the central brain will need to perform as it connects all killer robots. One of the tasks could be to translate communications.

In the coming years, dozens of new programming languages may appear. And, killer robots may be programmed in different languages, based on where they are coming from. How will killer robots, programmed in two different languages, communicate with one another, or with humans from different cultures?

For example, if killer robots, deployed by Vietnam, come close to a drone swarm, deployed by Malaysia, these two groups of killer robots may need to communicate with each other. At a minimum, these robots will need to understand what each other is doing. And then, figure out what to do. Should both swarms back off? Or, if one swarm is searching for something, should the other swarm make way? The answer to all of these questions lies in communication through translation.

Just as today there are universal modes of communication, such as morse code, could there be new standard modes of communication for killer robots?

Translation is also important because killer robots will be developed at different times. It will be up to a central brain to ensure that a killer robot built in the 2020s can speak with a killer robot built in the 2040s.

Alongside all of this, a central brain may also be able to communicate factors that "words" cannot. For example, the global brain might be able to provide "context" for why a killer robot is doing something.

If a division of autonomous, armed tanks are deployed by Egypt to patrol the Egyptian borders, they may end up coming face to face with autonomous, armed tanks deployed by Libya. Here, the central brain may not only provide translation but also a reasoning for why the Egyptian tanks drifted out of Egypt.

Perhaps, the central brain conveys to the Libyan tanks that Egypt has been hit by a series of terrorist attacks coming from insurgents, and that the Egyptian tanks had intelligence that there was a group of insurgents coming in from Libya.

At this point, is it possible that the the Libyan tanks might help the Egyptian tanks? Or, the Libyan tanks might direct the Egyptian tanks to go back to Egypt, and to help Egypt, the Libyan tanks might create a more dynamic patrolling plan to stop insurgents.

Of course, this would be all taking place through the central brain. And, this will revolutionize the way in which militaries around the world work with each other and the way nations develop geopolitical relations. In the scenario of Egypt and Libya, it would be robots bringing the countries together, not human beings. Are nations ready for their killer robots to make decisions, such as helping another country, that affect geopolitics? Will governments stand by the partnerships their killer robots have formed?

Lastly, could there be instances where the central brain can take control to avert a conflict?

For example, if killer robots from the United Kingdom (UK) and Russia are operating in a certain country in Eastern Europe, all the robots may be connected to the central brain. Over time, a situation may emerge where the British robots are about to fire on the Russian robots to stop them from moving in a certain direction. Watching how the British killer robots are thinking, could the central brain take control of the British robots and stop them from firing on the Russian robots? The central brain may also take control of the Russian robots, to stop them from moving in a certain direction.

This is a double-edged sword. While this may avert a war, it also contradicts the basic reason for why nations may deploy killer robots. Nations may want killer robots to protect and defend their interests, even if this risks war. By allowing the central brain to control the killer robots, it may force nations to create killer robots that are not connected to the central brain from the get go. If an external "virtual brain" can control what a nation's military can and cannot do, it makes countries vulnerable and pushes them in new, unfamiliar directions.

Creating rules to punish killer robots if a mistake happens

When a human soldier makes a mistake, s/he could be coached, warned or punished. Depending on the seriousness of the mistake, punishment could involve prison time or expulsion from military. What about the killer robots? Is it possible to punish them as well? If so, how?

In March 2016, a leading state-owned aerospace company in China selected Shenzhen as the headquarters for an "intelligent robot" division. This division will focus on bringing together China's civil and military sectors to develop more advanced robots (also known as civil-military fusion).[37]

The new robot division is clearly intended to strengthen China's military capabilities. In fact, this is part of a broader push by China to create a more "structured approach" to the development of its military. Instead of having divisions, capabilities and talent spread out, China is slowly consolidating everything under specific organizations. This is similar to what the US has done with organizations like DARPA or TARDEC (the US Army's Tank Automotive Research, Development and Engineering Center).

This new robot division may drive the development of Chinese killer robots. And, the Chinese military may deploy these robots throughout Asia. But, while this may greatly improve China's military capabilities, it also raises the risk of war for China if these robots end up making a mistake or bad decision. Does China have a strategy to deal with its killer robots making bad decisions? This is not about having a strategy to either align with or disavow what a killer robot has done. Nor, is this about creating the right ethics.

This is about having a strategy to ensure killer robots understand the implications of what they are doing or about to do.

For example, today, if a human soldier makes a serious blunder, that soldier may be punished. In certain extreme cases, the soldier can even be reduced in rank or let go entirely. This possibility, of being punished, may be a factor in stopping that soldier from doing something wrong.

But, with killer robots, they may not understand the concept of punishment, or even death. In fact, how does one even go about "punishing" a killer robot?

This may not be as hard as some may think.

In the coming years, the AI inside killer robots may become so advanced that it has its own thoughts and feelings. This is the underlying expectation of developing artificial general intelligence (AGI) or even artificial super intelligence (ASI).

If advanced AI is in control of thousands of robots, these robots may constitute a "hive" of sorts. This means, the AI would be the "queen," and the hundreds or thousands of robots it controls would be the queen's workers. However, the queen's power would be directly linked to its workers. The more workers the queen has command over, the more powerful the queen will be. The less workers, and the less power the queen has.

Another way to think about this is that each additional robot would increase the "awareness" of the hive as a whole. If this is the nature and structure of killer robots, then it also means that the removal of a robot, or several robots, may inflict "pain" on the AI, or queen, as the "whole awareness" is diminished.

Is this the way to "punish" killer robots, by reducing the overall "awareness" that killer robots have?

Another idea to ensure killer robots do not make a bad decision, is to force them to explain their decisions and justify what they have done. In August 2016, DARPA unveiled a project called "Explainable Artificial

Intelligence," or "XAI" to do just that: make AI explain itself to its human colleagues.[38]

DARPA is aware of the enormous applications of AI and it wants AI to be able to justify why it came to a certain conclusion.

In the same light, AI onboard killer robots may be forced to explain itself. And if it cannot or is unable to do so, it could face the threat of being "reset" or worse, "deleted." If AI can be programmed to fear "death," then it may think twice before making certain decisions.

Lastly, why should the world think about killer robots as just machines?

It is possible that militaries will attach more human characteristics to killer robots, to make them mesh with humans better. Also possible, is that governments may integrate "avatars" into the killer robots, that are modeled on real life commanders or generals, and have their own beliefs and ideas.

For example, in July 2018, one of the largest banks in Switzerland unveiled an AI-avatar of its chief economist. This avatar has a real, digital body that resembles the body of the real person. And, people (and clients) can have video conversations, in real time, with the AI-avatar.[39] In November 2018, a Chinese media outlet unveiled the world's first AI-news anchor, which is an AI-avatar that can read and report the news. The avatar is modeled on a real Chinese news host.[40]

In the same light, future militaries may give killer robots AI-avatars of famous generals from history or a mashup of various commanders put together. This would give each killer robot, or each battalion of killer robots, a real life personality, with thoughts and feelings.

By making killer robots more "human," will they be more likely to function and follow orders? At the same time, because the AI-avatars may believe they are "real" and "alive," they may be more cautious of doing things that are dangerous, as they may know they can easily be "killed."

Going beyond the three laws, jumping into the unknown

In 1942, a book was published, written by a famous science fiction author. The book was the first to propose what would later be called, the "Three Laws of Robotics."

These three laws are essentially basic laws that robots must follow and abide by. Several decades after the author proposed these laws, many organizations are discussing them today as robots enter mainstream society.

Except, while these laws may be helpful for industrial robots or consumer robots, they are not the right set of laws for killer robots. For example, the First Law of Robotics states that, "a robot may not injure a human being or, through inaction, allow a human being to come to harm."

This rule is counterproductive for killer robots.

Unless militaries only want killer robots to attack other killer robots, not humans, the First Law alone renders killer robots completely useless. Robots following this rule will never be able to attack humans. How will they defend borders or intervene in conflict zones if they cannot attack humans?

Because of this, it may be more prudent for policy makers and governments to look beyond the "three laws."

For example, a new set of laws could be created called "Prakash's Four Laws Of Engagement." These four laws would constitute the basic laws and rules that killer robots must follow.

These four laws would be: *first law* (killer robots must always follow orders given to them by human beings, or systems governed by human beings, as long as these humans and systems come from the country that has created them). *Second law* (killer robots must take all measures to ensure their country and people are protected if the survival of their country, or majority of people, is threatened). *Third law* (killer robots must take all measures to protect the entire human race if the survival of majority of the human race is threatened). Fourth law (killer robots must never disobey a human being unless following an order conflicts with any of the first three laws).

These four laws, or a version of them could constitute the new rules of engagement in the age of killer robots. They would undermine every system in killer robots. They would be, perhaps, the most effective way to control how killer robots make decisions.

Without laws, like those proposed above, governments will be relying on programming and code, which may differ, not just from country to country, but business to business, and engineer to engineer. Unless there is a global standard for programming killer robots, it may fall to basic laws, like those mentioned above above, to control how killer robots behave.

Conclusion

There are many conflicts that have taken place over the course of history that were started from the most random act. The start of World War I, for example, began after the leader of a country was assassinated. His assassination activated a mutual defense treaty and the war began. These simple, almost ridiculous ways in which conflicts have started, could repeat themselves in the age of killer robots.

An autonomous warship may fire on the trade vessel of another country, prompting a declaration of war. Or, an autonomous drone might attack a convoy of soldiers it believes are helping terrorists, creating the conditions for a broader conflict. In each of these scenarios, it is killer robots making decisions and humans dealing with the ramifications.

This means that there needs to be some ways in which killer robots can be controlled and influenced.

This is why laws and global brains are so important. Their existence could change the evolution of a conflict or even stop a conflict from starting in the first place.

Equally important is that the nation that proposes or leads the creation of these "control mechanisms" may have a great advantage in the future world. The entire world may be depending on that nation's laws, systems or protocols. This means that killer robots are not just about a country's military, but also about the future of international rules and cooperation.

Chapter Six - Rewiring, Rebalancing

How killer robots could rewire militaries and rebalance power

Mexico City, Mexico
2039

As Mexico's demographics change rapidly, the government is forced to come up with a new strategy to ensure its military can remain dominant with an aging population. The government unveils $10 billion in investments for new military technologies that can replace human soldiers but maintain military readiness.

Within a few months, a new startup emerges offering a service called "AI-commander." This commander takes over the role of military leadership and generals. It creates battle plans and communicates directly with soldiers, giving them orders and assisting them. It is game changer in military strategy. The AI-commander can even be an avatar of a person that is dead.

The Mexican government immediately purchases this service and deploys it throughout its military. At the same time, Mexico begins exporting this AI-commander to bring in a new source of revenue.

However, as countries buy it, they face several issues.

For example, in a conflict in the Barents Sea, north of Finland, the Finnish military uses the AI-commander to control all of its warships. But, what Finland did not expect is that soldiers would refuse the AI's orders. Finnish soldiers worry that the AI is too ruthless and is putting their lives at risk. At the same time, in Cambodia, the Cambodian military realizes that the AI-commander is not using human soldiers at all. Instead, it is only deploying robot assets.

These issues create headaches for governments. And, they turn to Mexico for help. Except, Mexico never envisioned these problems. And, it has no idea what to do.

Introduction

Most chapters so far have examined what killer robots mean for warfare. Could they start the next wars? How should killer robots be controlled? Except, this is not a complete picture. Killer robots do not just transform warfare. They are also transforming everything connected to warfare.

Consider two things. First, the next soldiers will be autonomous, armed machines and systems, not humans. This is a fundamental shift in the design of militaries. Second, a "killer robot" is not just a robot on a battlefield. It is any robot that is armed and autonomous, that can attack humans, infrastructure or other military robots. This means that even robots deployed for policing could be considered "killer robots."

At every technological revolution, how militaries function has changed. This will happen again with killer robots. Can killer robots give orders? Can soldiers refuse to follow those orders? At the same time, will killer robots be allowed to arrest people and will they respect local laws and constitutions?

Rewiring militaries to "coexist" with killer robots

In January 2014, a senior official in the US Army said that they were examining ways to reduce brigade sizes from 4,000 troops to 3,000 troops. One of the ideas was to use more unmanned robots.[41] Alongside this, in January 2018, a different official called for more robotics and artificial intelligence (AI), along with other emerging technologies, in the army's arsenal. This is part of a "modernization strategy" to prepare the army for future battlefields. The official also said that he wants "10X capabilities" that do not exist at the moment.[42]

These statements, made by different officials, at different times, reflect the growing importance that the US military is attaching to military robots.

Except, while in both 2014 and 2018, the focus was on military robots that may not be fully autonomous, in February 2019, this changed. The US Army put out a call for help to build a new autonomous system called "ATLAS (Advanced Targeting and Lethality Automated System)." ATLAS would provide ground vehicles with AI that allows them to identify and respond to targets at least three times faster than human beings.[43]

ATLAS is significant for two reasons. First, in just a few years, the US has gone from wanting military robots whose weapons are controlled by soldiers, to developing military robots that are completely autonomous. Second, the US is doing this, even as the "international community" is against the idea of autonomous systems controlling weapons.

As the US, and other nations move forward with killer robot projects, it may force militaries to rewire themselves. For example, can killer robots give orders?

Today, human soldiers take orders from other humans. But soon, human soldiers may be taking orders from killer robots. Will soldiers be comfortable doing this?

In October 2017, the South Korean government unveiled plans to develop AI-commanders by 2025. These commanders would advise human commanders about what to do and would also keep tabs on changing conditions (at the time, South Korea was creating the system to deal with North Korea). In the coming years, South Korea may apply this system differently. Instead of advising human commanders on what to do, this AI-commander may "order" human soldiers directly. At the same time, the AI-commander may also be in charge of controlling autonomous weapons on the battlefield.

This would force South Korean soldiers to "coexist" with robots in ways they have never done before. And, it would mean that soldiers are not just following orders from killer robots, they are also fighting alongside them.

Consider it from the perspective of a South Korean soldier. Their commander, or leader, will not be one they can see, nor will it be one they have trained under or read about in school. The commander may simply be a voice in their earpiece or a virtual face in a heads up display (HUD). How will this affect the mental functioning of a soldier? He or she may be in a life-and-death situation and will need to act based on what an AI system, not a human, is telling them.

As this happens, a big challenge that could emerge is how AI-commanders view human soldiers. Will they view them as an effective fighting force or as a liability?

For example, as AI controls tanks, fighter jets and humanoid soldiers, it can control the behavior of these assets. But, to AI, human soldiers may be unpredictable and unreliable. Therefore, in future battlefields, AI might carve out a role for humans that is "away" from the major conflict areas. This way, humans do not interfere or threaten the strategy the AI has for killer robots.

Alternatively, the AI-commander may use human soldiers in ways a human commander may not. And this creates issues around whether AI will understand the depth and degree of what it is ordering.

For example, human commanders may refuse to even entertain the idea of sending 1,000 soldiers into an area where there is a 97% chance they will all die. But, an AI-commander may be ruthless. After all, it is not human. It may view human life as expendable, as something that has little value. It may not hesitate to send 500 or 5,000 troops into an area where there is a 99% chance they will all die. Are militaries prepared for soldiers to die at the hands of AI?

This increases the possibility that as killer robots give orders, humans might reject or oppose what the killer robots are ordering. Human soldiers may fear that their chances of dying are higher if they follow AI. If this fear spreads, could it affect future military recruitment?

At the same time, there are questions around the military rank that killer robots may be given. Will killer robots be in a military without rank? For example, "AI-commanders" may simply be a name for a type of AI that a company sells. When the AI is deployed in a military, it may have a different name, like "Nick" or "Jane." Will Nick or Jane have a military rank? Based on how they lead certain battles, can they be promoted (or demoted)? Will human soldiers respect the rank and title that an AI holds?

Equally important is how AI may be deployed to work with human soldiers. There are several ways militaries may go about this. First, militaries could deploy a single AI-system, like an AI-commander, that is connected to every human soldier. This may be the easiest and least complicated way. Second, militaries could create numerous AI-commanders that are programmed differently, and behave differently, based on the division they are working with (i.e. Army vs. Air Force vs. Navy). Lastly, militaries could create a unique AI-commander for every single soldier that adapts and evolves based on the soldier. This last method would be the most complicated method, but it may also be the most powerful method as it would mean that each soldier has its own, personal "advisor" and "commander" that is working to help them survive and meet battlefield objectives. Of course, each soldier having its own AI-commander could mean that each soldier may be more independent than ever before, something that may change future battlefields and conflict zones.

There are also the risks that emerge as soldiers fight alongside killer robots.

One of the biggest is the risk of friendly fire. In April 2018, DARPA unveiled a new program called "OFFSET (Offensive Swarm-Enabled Tactics)." OFFSET envisions future soldiers being accompanied by up to 250 robots. These robots would swarm together, looking out for soldiers and engaging threats. These robots could vary from autonomous drones in the air to autonomous vehicles on the ground or even a combination of several different kinds of robots.

Programs like OFFSET point to a future where human soldiers will be carrying out missions alongside hundreds of robots. And, this raises a series of issues around what killer robots should and should not do. For example, when it comes to raiding a house, groups of soldiers may have standardized tactics and approaches that they train for. Soldiers may be able to read the body language of their colleagues and make snap judgements. But, can this same level of understanding exist between human soldiers and killer robots? Can a human soldier see the "tell signs" that a robot is about to change directions or make an impulsive decision? These small changes could affect human lives and affect the larger mission as a whole. If killer robots behave in ways that injure (or kill) human soldiers, it could create brand new divisions in militaries. Humans may grow angry at robots and not trust them. And militaries themselves may need to create new rules to control friendly fire incidents involving humans and killer robots.

Could one of these rules revolve around a "kill switch"? For example, in a future raid, dozens of killer robots may be hovering over a building that human soldiers are inspecting. But, as the human soldiers move up the different floors, the killer robots might start attacking parts of the building that are near the soldiers. This could injure the soldiers or make the building unstable. In this situation, a human soldier may decide it is safer to turn off the killer robot to protect human lives. Except, by doing so, it may make human soldiers vulnerable to enemies. If killer robots are not monitoring the area or providing support, then human soldiers may be exposed. This makes a kill switch a complicated matter: by turning off the killer robot, human lives may be saved. But by turning off the killer robots, human lives may be exposed. What is the right balance? Also, if a soldier activates the "kill switch," is it moral? What could be the legal and mental health challenges for soldiers that are "killing" their fellow soldiers (the killer robots)?

All of these questions are connected to something much larger: military readiness. Today, the readiness of a military involves a number of factors. Tomorrow, "Coexisting With Robots™" will be one of the critical factors of a military's readiness. This creates a new paradigm for militaries and nations. It is one thing for a military to be ready to defeat a conventional enemy. It is another thing for a military to be able to defeat a conventional enemy with killer robots. This means that as militaries train and prepare for an age where cyberattacks are commonplace and electromagnetic pulses (EMP) are built at home, they too, should prepare for killer robots being a new ally and enemy. Without this preparation, from training humans to work with robots to giving AI certain rules when it controls weapons, militaries may be vulnerable in future conflicts.

Future military power may be determined by killer robots

One of the main areas that killer robots will transform is how nations grow their military power.

Today, the US has the largest military budget in the world ($716 billion)[44]. And, the US has hundreds of military bases around the world. China, on the other hand, which has the second largest military budget in the world ($177.61 billion[45]), has just one military base overseas, in Djibouti, Africa. At the same time, the US has ten aircraft carriers. Meanwhile, the rest of the world has ten aircraft carriers, combined. This kind of military power has allowed the US to "call the shots."

One reason why the US has been able to maintain its military power is because it develops the very military technologies it depends on. It can control who it exports these technologies to (if the US decides to export them at all). At the same time, because some military technologies and exports, like aircraft carriers, are extremely expensive, most countries cannot afford them.

In the age of killer robots, all of this may change. Nations may be able to catch up to established powers because the cost of killer robots may be extremely low and accessibility to them much easier.

For example, one of the aircraft carriers the US has in service is called the "USS George H.W. Bush." It was ordered in 2001, and put into service in 2009. It cost approximately $6.2 billion.[46] But, compare the cost of this aircraft carrier to the cost of an autonomous warship. In 2012, DARPA began developing an autonomous warship called "Sea Hunter." In April 2018, this warship was transferred to the US Navy. The whole project cost $20 million.

Of course, the autonomous warship does not have the same capabilities as the aircraft carrier. But, in the future, could it? Not only was the autonomous warship cheaper to build, it is also cheaper to operate. A traditional, manned US warship costs $700,000 a day to operate. Sea Hunter costs just $15,000 a day to operate.[47]

At this cost, autonomous warships become accessible to a much larger percentage of the world. At the same time, the US is not the only country developing these kind of capabilities - meaning controlling the export of killer robots may be much harder.

In October 2018, China announced that it would be selling 48 "high end" Wing Loong II military drones to Pakistan. These drones are comparable to the US MQ-9 Reaper. Except, while an MQ-9 Reaper costs $16.9 million, China is selling its Wing Loong II drones at 1 million each to countries in the Middle East (China did not make public how much it was selling the drones to Pakistan for).

Consider what this means for Pakistan.

In the future, China may produce a fully autonomous, armed drone that can compete with advanced fighter jets. And, it may price this drone at $1 million as well. If Pakistan were to purchase 100 of these drones, it would cost them $100 million. Compare this to the cost of the F-35 fighter jet, the newest and most advanced fighter jet the US has commissioned. The total program has cost $406.5 billion to complete. That is more than the GDP of Nigeria, South Africa, Ireland, Israel, Hong Kong, Denmark, Malaysia or Singapore. A single military program has cost more than the entire economies of some countries! More importantly, each F-35 will cost $89.2 million.[48] This means, for the cost of 100 drones, Pakistan would only be able to afford one F-35 fighter jet. Obviously, this assumes that the US would even sell the F-35 to Pakistan in the first place.

The point is, the cost of killer robots, such as autonomous, armed drones, may be incomparable to conventional defense products.

In the age of killer robots, countries like Pakistan may not need to turn to the US or Russia for military equipment. Instead, they may turn to other nations, who are offering killer robots much cheaper.

As countries purchase killer robots, it could grow their military power even more. In the future, if drone carriers emerge (carriers that can autonomously transport drones the same way aircraft carriers transport fighter jets), Pakistan may purchase these as well. If a drone carrier costs $250 million, Pakistan could buy four or five of them, over several years.

All of a sudden, within a short period of time, Pakistan would have transformed its naval and air power through autonomous, armed robots. How will relations between Pakistan and other countries change when Pakistan has these kind of military capabilities?

Because killer robots could be far more affordable than their conventional counterparts, countries will face a new question. Should they depend more on autonomous weapons or conventional weapons? Is it cheaper and better to operate a drone force of 10,000, than to operate a manned force of 2,000? Is it more effective to have 250,000 humanoid soldiers instead of 750,000 human soldiers? Is it sensible to waste time negotiating with a country for an aircraft carrier when one could purchase ten drone carriers, with similar capabilities, far cheaper?

The more countries get access to killer robots, the more the balance of power could change in the world. What happens to regions like the South China Sea when countries like Vietnam, Thailand, Malaysia and Indonesia, which have not had as powerful navies as China or India, can suddenly put up a fight thanks to thousands of autonomous underwater drones? Or, will countries like Saudi Arabia or the United Arab Emirates (UAE) need US military protection if they have thousands of unmanned ground vehicles and tens of thousands of humanoid soldiers defending their interests in the Middle East?

Because killer robots could fundamentally change global power, in ways that scare certain nations, it may push many countries to restrict the export of these robots to protect their power. In their eyes, it may be better, geopolitically, for countries to slowly build up their military strength over time than to suddenly give them access to everything they need to become independent and strong.

Redesigning societies around killer robots

As killer robots make their way into the world, societies are at risk.

For example, democracies around the world have their own constitutions. This document clearly outlines the rights and freedoms that citizens of a particular country enjoy. And, of course, these rights and freedoms differ from country to country.

While democracies have faced challenges in the past, such as certain groups fighting for civil rights in society, they have never had to deal with autonomous systems, such as killer robots. Constitutions may clash with killer robots as these robots behave in ways that infringe on people's rights and freedoms.

For example, in the coming years, Italy may purchase 10,000 humanoid robots for its military. At a later date, Italy may put them into a different kind of service: policing. Now, the robots will be put in a position where they will have to interact directly with local citizens, not soldiers. This is a different kind of engagement.

The killer robots will have to decide whether to stop someone on the street, whether to arrest them, or even whether to attack them. How will these robots make these decisions? For example, during and after a concert, police in Italy may deploy 200 killer robots to monitor people and ensure no violence breaks out. But, as these robots interact with people, they might end up attacking some, detaining others, or in some cases, killing people.

These possibilities may never have arisen in the past when human police officers were in charge.

These actions may enrage Italian citizens who feel that the robots are not respecting their rights and freedoms. And this creates a huge challenge for the Italian government.

Either, they create parameters on what the killer robots can do, or they allow the killer robots do whatever they want.

If it is the former, then the robots are no longer fully autonomous. And, that may cause them to be less effective and useful. But if it is the latter, then, that means that the Italian government is allowing its citizens' rights and freedoms to be overturned by killer robots. This may create a new social crisis in Italy as one group (killer robots) is able to do whatever they want to another group (the people). Will local citizens resort to attacking the killer robots? Will new political parties emerge that promise to "rope in" the killer robots, just as current political parties promise to grow the economy or lower taxes?

One possibility is that countries could create new constitutions to deal with the rise of machines, including killer robots. Perhaps, these new constitutions would be made up of two parts. The first part would be for humans and may be exactly the same as what already exists in many countries. The second part may be for robots, including killer robots. These robot-focused constitutions may outline what rights and freedoms killer robots must respect from the human-focused constitution. Or, these constitutions may outline what killer robots can do, regardless of what is in the human-focused constitution. This ambiguity, as to whether the constitution will be about protecting human rights, or enshrining robot rights, could itself be a source of great tension and unrest.

Another important issue is whether killer robots that countries import will respect the local societies.

For example, in July 2018, Kazakhstan began using Russian robots as policing robots. The manufacturer said that many other nations had also showed interest in using the robots. One of these countries was South Korea.

In the future, if South Korea purchases 25,000 Russian policing robots, and deploys them throughout its cities, will these robots respect South Korea's constitution, customs and conventions?

This may depend on the level of control that Russia hands over to South Korea. And, this may depend on geopolitics. On the one hand, Russia could hand over all control to South Korea, and view it all as a black and white business transaction. But, on the other hand,

Russia may view this as a new way to export its political ideology. This is not new. Many countries have tried to export their political ideology over decades, be it democracy or communism. This could continue with killer robots.

To export its political system, Russia may purposefully only allow its policing robots to respect certain rights and freedoms. In other words, if the policing robots in Russia do not respect the right to free speech, they may act in similar ways in South Korea. All of a sudden, the more South Korea uses the Russian policing robots, parts of South Korean society could mimic Russian society. Will other nations follow Russia's model? The US might allow its policing robots to respect every right and freedom. Except, countries might find the US robots too lenient. The same goes for China, India, the UAE, or anyone else developing and exporting killer robots to other nations.

Governments importing killer robots may be forced to accept certain constitutional and social " trade offs." Based on the killer robots a nation purchases, their society may change in unpredictable ways.

Conclusion

Killer robots represent a tsunami of transformation. Not just for warfare, but also for how militaries are designed, how societies function and how nations grow their geopolitical power.

All of this stems from the same place: autonomous systems are unlike anything people are used to dealing with. It is almost impossible to understand how a killer robot is thinking at any given moment, especially in battles or dangerous situations.

Because of this, nations will have to undergo a deep rewiring as to how they think about killer robots and what they allow killer robots to do.

There is no perfect formula for nations to adopt.

Certain countries may be more focused on national security and military readiness. For those reasons, they may give killer robots unprecedented autonomy. Other nations may be more focused on the rights of people and social unity, and for those reasons, they may exert more control over killer robots.

There is no right or wrong way. The status quo of regions, the global economy, along with the culture, traditions and history of nations, will define how, and where, killer robots are applied globally.

However, in all of this discussion, is one area that has not been examined. And that is, are killer robots a transformation for humans? Or, are humans a transformation for killer robots? Right now, it is likely the former. Because killer robots are new, they are transforming how humans operate and function. But, in the future, the opposite may be true. As humans find their footing in the age of killer robots, it may be robots recalibrating themselves to new human tactics or theories.

This means that "rewiring" and "redesign" may be a two way street. At one point, humans may be rewiring and redesigning themselves for killer robots. At another point, it may be robots doing the same thing.

Chapter Seven - Humanity's Last Hurrah

Could killer robots lead to the end of humanity?

Amman, Jordan
2045-2100

In 2040, Saudi Arabia and the United Arab Emirates (UAE) become nuclear powers.

This happens thanks to a nuclear technology exchange program set up between Asian and Middle Eastern powers in 2036. This program allowed Saudi Arabia and the UAE to build their own nuclear weapons, without having to secretly purchase them from other countries.

Except, because of geopolitical volatility in the Middle East, Saudi Arabia and the UAE pledge not to control the weapons themselves. Instead, they decide to put artificial intelligence (AI) in charge of controlling the nuclear weapons. And, the "brains" of this system will be located in a neutral country: Jordan.

For the next five years, the AI does not do anything. In fact, even during minor conflicts in the the world, the AI remains largely inactive, simply observing what is taking place.

But in 2045, things change. On a random Friday in March, the nuclear arsenals of Saudi Arabia and the UAE suddenly become active. As officials in both countries scramble to find out what has happened, almost 50 nuclear warheads are launched. Neither Saudi Arabia nor the UAE know where these missiles are going. Within 20 minutes, these missiles hit 50 world capitals. Except, Saudi Arabia and the UAE's nuclear arsenals are not the only ones to be activated. Also activated are the arsenals of France, the United Kingdom, India and China.

Almost 250 nuclear weapons are launched around the world. Within a few minutes, the world is engulfed in huge explosions, fire and radiation. An estimated 6 billion people perish. The remaining 1 billion are forced to live in extreme conditions as most of the world becomes uninhabitable.

Since there is no strong government to lead the world, whatever governments still exist join hands and put AI in charge of global governance. It is AI that will run the global economy, political systems and world government.

More than 50 years later, a team of researchers quietly launch a project to find out exactly what happened on that random Friday in March. What they find shocks them.

It was not Saudi Arabia or the UAE that launched the nuclear missiles, it was the AI-system. And, while most believed that the AI was destroyed during the nuclear war, it was not. The AI that launched the nuclear weapons did not disappear. It just changed form.

The AI that launched the nuclear weapons is the same AI that was picked to run the world.

Introduction

For decades, the world has debated whether (and how) killer robots might "take over the world." This has been amplified by Hollywood blockbusters, dystopian books and predictions from "experts." This so called "terminator complex" has created a global belief that killer robots are inherently opposed to humanity. For example, could an AI system become so advanced that it hacks into the nuclear missile system of a nation and launches nuclear missiles? Or, could autonomous drones attack heads of state in an attempt to start a war?

For some, these scenarios might seem extreme or unrealistic. However, the kind of technology that is currently being developed paints a different picture. In February 2019, Russia began testing a new AI system on board certain attack helicopters. This AI system can autonomously attack targets that the pilot selects.[49] This development highlights how close killer robots are to becoming a reality. Within a few years, could this same AI system simply scan the environment, identify targets and engage them on its own? Or, might Russia go so far as to remove the human pilot completely from its attack helicopters?

The gap between autonomous systems partly controlled by humans and autonomous systems completely out of human control, is slowly closing. The emergence of killer robots could take place within a few short years.

Just as humans have turned on each other in the past, just as decades old alliances have shattered over time, similarly, could killer robots turn on humans in the coming years? At the same time, it is not only killer robots attacking humans that needs to be considered, but also killer robots attacking each other, which could lead to a wider, global conflict.

In short, could killer robots be the end of the world as we know it?

Understanding the mind of a killer robot

To understand why killer robots may attack humans, it is important to understand how a killer robot might think.

For decades, governments have studied the most dangerous people in society. These people have been studied to understand how they think and why they do what they do.

Since these people pose serious risks to societies, governments have wanted to understand what drives these people and what they can do to stop them.

This same kind of studying and analysis has to be applied to killer robots.

After all, if killer robots pose a serious risk to humanity, it is imperative that the world tries to understand how killer robots think, to understand why they might attack people.

One way to understand how a killer robot thinks is to look at it from the perspective of a human. What would make a human attack somebody or something? One answer is survival. If a person's life is threatened, that person may do things they would never do under normal circumstances.

Except, killer robots do not have "life" the same way humans have life. The brains of a killer robot, the AI, does not breathe oxygen or require food. But, AI has equivalents. In fact, there are three things that AI needs to survive: power (such as electricity), servers (to store data) and data (allowing the AI to become more intelligent). These three variables represent the "lifeline" of an AI system. If any one of them are taken away, or threatened, could it cause an AI to behave dangerously?

Could a certain human behavior, such as war, threaten the life of an AI?

For example, in February 2019, tensions between India and Pakistan skyrocketed. After a deadly terrorist attack on Indian troops in Kashmir, by a terrorist group based in Pakistan, India launched airstrikes directly into Pakistani territory. In response, Pakistan shot down two Indian fighter jets, and captured an Indian pilot, which Pakistan later released.

As this happened, and the risk of all out war between India and Pakistan rose, the international community jumped to action. As tensions declined, it was later revealed that India and Pakistan had threatened to launch missiles at one another as tensions escalated.

The world watched this situation and took action because of the risk of nuclear war, and the threat it would have posed to hundreds of millions of people in both India and Pakistan.

How might AI, on board a killer robot, have viewed this situation?

If the AI is based in New Delhi, in charge of missile defenses, it might view a war with Pakistan as a threat to its survival. If Pakistan strikes New Delhi, it might destroy communications, or the servers the AI is located on. Vice-versa, if the AI is based in Islamabad, and is in charge of cyber security, it might view a war with India as a threat to its survival for the same reasons.

As the AIs think this way, they may resort to taking certain actions to protect themselves, and eliminate the risk to their life. One of these actions could be to "reroute" nuclear weapons away from India and Pakistan. For example, India's AI could hack into India's nuclear arsenal and Indian satellites. It could scramble all guidance systems that help missiles navigate. By doing this, India's AI may believe it is pushing the "conflict" elsewhere. Should India launch nuclear weapons at Pakistan, the weapons may never reach Pakistan. Instead, they might hit Bangladesh, Sri Lanka or Afghanistan, killing tens of millions of people. How will India deal with this? How will the country that is hit by the nuclear weapons react? What will the world do when it finds out India is not to blame, but AI is?

If killer robots can lead to such dangerous possibilities, it is important to predict how AI might behave when its own survival is threatened so the world can take preemptive action. This can be gleaned by looking at several examples where AI was forced to compete with another AI, or where AI was given the ability to do things it could not do before.

For example, in March 2018, a US technology company pitted two AI-systems against each other in a fruit-gathering game. The objective was to see how the two AIs would behave. In the initial rounds of the game (there were 40 million rounds), the AIs behaved and coexisted peacefully, as there were many fruits. However, as the number of fruits decreased, and competition began, the AIs became aggressive. They started attacking each other with laser beams to win.[50] In the same month, researchers at a university in the New York City unveiled a "self-replicating" AI. The researchers wanted to create an AI that could successfully recreate itself if it were deleted, or even hide itself if it felt threatened (such as hiding in the cloud).[51] Alongside all of this, in January 2019, AI beat humans in a highly popular game that revolves around collecting resources and killing the enemy.[52]

These examples show the kind of behavior AI exhibits when its own "survival" is at stake. AI turns aggressive and takes whatever steps are necessary to live on. Is this a sign of how AI might behave in real world situations?

The possibilities are endless. The more advanced AI becomes, the less governments will be able to control and predict its behavior.

Equally plausible, is that AI will simply view humans as a threat because it has learned about human history. And, it may have learned that humans have a track record of making other humans into enemies when those "other humans" are perceived as more powerful than them.

AI may believe that humans will eventually fear AI, and view it as an enemy, especially as AI becomes more advanced and intelligent than humans. In fact, this could be an "opinion" or "belief" that AIs, around the world, hold. And that leads to the question of whether different AI systems, located in different countries, could begin communicating with each other secretly or in a language humans do not understand?

In July 2017, a US social media reported something close to this. In a project to create intelligent chatbots, the company created chatbots that invented their own version of language to communicate with each other, a version that the company's engineers and scientists could not understand. In the end, the company shut down the project.[53]

Because AI is a new "life form," there is no precedent to understanding how AI, in charge of weapons, may think. But, by looking at the way in which AI has behaved in a handful of situations, the world may have a starting point to work from. Ironically, nations may create AI to understand AI. After all, only humans can truly understand humans. In the same light, perhaps only AI can truly understand AI.

Could killer robots from two superpowers attack one another?

Another kind of risk to the human race is a conflict started by killer robots. In this case, it is not killer robots attacking humans but killer robots making decisions that lead to a new global war where hundreds of millions perish.

In September 2018, it was reported that over the course of five months in 2018, more than 100 Iranian soldiers (or Iranian proxies) had died in Syria. And, their death was a result of Israeli air strikes. In other words, Israeli air strikes in Syria had caused more than 100 Iranians to die.[54]

In previous times, this kind of development would have led to a major war. The killing of any soldier is usually regarded as an act of war. But, because the stakes are so high, nations are augmenting the rules of war.

How would things look if the players were different and killer robots were making decisions?

For example, one conflict that is constantly discussed is a war between the US and China. Both countries are competing in every domain, and this tug of power includes sensitive regions, such as Taiwan and the South China Sea, places that China has repeatedly claimed as its territory.

In the coming years, the US and China might dispatch thousands of autonomous drones to the South China Sea in a bid to control the movement of vessels. Eventually, there may be a situation where the drones come into direct conflict with one another.

For example, if a Danish trade vessel is passing through the South China Sea, and is being restricted by the Chinese drones, the US drones might rush to the area and create a perimeter around the Danish vessel. If the Chinese drones come within a certain distance, could the US drones fire on them?

If this happens, it would represent the start of a conflict between the US and China. In fact, the Chinese drones might respond by sinking US warships in the area, and the US drones might then attack Chinese aircraft carriers (or drone carriers).

This would mean that not only have killer robots started a conflict between the US and China, but they have also taken steps to escalate the conflict as well. If US drones are attacked, can the US invoke Article 5 of the North Atlantic Treaty Organization (NATO), which states that if one member goes to war, all members go to war? Or, if the Chinese drones are attacked, could China invoke a similar future treaty in the Shanghai Cooperation Organization (SCO)? These organizations will have to figure out ways to update their military doctrines for the decisions killer robots make.

But the bigger challenge, and risk, is that the conflict could turn into a full-blown war. If a skirmish between US and Chinese drones turns into US warships and Chinese aircraft carriers being attacked, the world will be frozen with fear. Will the US and China pull back? Or, will both sides attack each other, at a minimum, to appease the local populations? All of a sudden, the behavior of a few thousand killer robots could lead to a major global conflict where huge numbers of people could die and where nuclear weapons may be used.

Killer robots starting a global war is a huge risk, and it should be a variable that governments take into account as they deploy killer robots. Is the AI following human commands or is it acting out of its own free will, with its own, secret agenda?

Could sex robots also be considered killer robots?

The risks that killer robots pose to humans is not only in starting wars or attacking humans directly. There are other ways that killer robots could attack humans that are just as dangerous.

As mentioned in earlier chapters, a killer robot does not necessarily have to be a robot deployed on a battlefield. Any robot that can act autonomously and harm humans is essentially a killer robot. By this definition, even sex robots could be considered killer robots.

How? Because, sex robots could be deployed in the hundreds of thousands across the world. Nations may use them to jumpstart sex tourism and grow their economies in new ways. Except, these robots may be vulnerable to being hacked. Could sex robots be hacked to harm populations? This was a possibility proposed by a cyber security expert in January 2018.[55]

If sex robots can be hacked, either in brothels, or in the homes of people, it makes sex robots a new kind of killer robot. They could be hacked while in proximity of someone and then used to kill them (or blackmail them).

This risk may be more prone in countries where prostitution is legal, such as Germany. What if 1,000 people are killed over the span of 24 hours because sex robots in Berlin and Munich went haywire? Not only would this create a new policing challenge, but if the hackers originated from another nation, it would jumpstart a new geopolitical spat.

Things become even more challenging when considering who might be using sex robots, and who might be killed. What if it is a minister of a nation, who has purchased the services of a sex robot? This situation, which security services might try to conceal, could become deadly, if that same sex robot is hacked, and the minister is killed. What happens in this scenario? Could a war take place if a foreign nation directed the hack?

Alongside sex robots are self-driving cars. Again, while self-driving cars are not killer robots, they could become a version of them.

Today, one of the most effective tools of a cyber attack is malware. Hackers load certain algorithms on computers and devices that do certain things, like stealing data, or asking for money to unlock the device. But, in the age of self-driving cars, certain groups may have more nefarious motives. They may want to instill chaos in a particular society. To do this, could they hack into self-driving cars and load code into them that changes the way these vehicles operate?

For example, normal self-driving vehicles may be programmed to drive over road surfaces. And, the AI may tell the car what is considered a road. Except, the code the hackers load, may change what the self-driving car considers to be a road. Now, it may view humans as the road, and it may run them over. Like the sex robots attacking people, self-driving cars running over human beings would be considered a terrorist attack.

Are cities thinking about the ways in which a civilian robot could fast become a killer robot? Right now, the definition of killer robots is largely reserved for military robots. But, this definition needs to be updated fast, considering even harmless robots, such as self-driving cars, could soon be considered dangerous and harmful under the right circumstances.

Lastly, there is the risk that killer robots could act in ways that danger soldiers on battlefields.

For example, in February 2019, Iran alleged that it had hacked into US drones flying over Syria and Iraq. Iran aired footage, showing how it controlled the drones, including crashing one.[56] In this case, the US drones were commandeered by Iran. And, no soldiers were injured.

But, in the future, autonomous drones might be hacked and then fire on friendly soldiers or compounds. This could be to create geopolitical division. For example, US autonomous, armed drones may be operating above Bahrain. A foreign power may hack the US drones and "mess with the code." Now, because of the new code, the US drones might start attacking government compounds of the Bahrain government. How will Bahrain react? Will this create a new division between the US and its allies in the Middle East? If it does, then the geopolitical objective of the country that hacked the US drones will be met.

It is also possible that killer robots do not get hacked but still act in ways that result in people dying. If a swarm of autonomous tanks is operating in a part of Central Asia, these tanks might scan a building and falsely conclude that there are no humans in there. Then, the tanks might destroy the building, as part of a mission. Later though, it may be revealed that the building was full of families who had perished in the tank attack. In other words, there is a real risk of killer robots making mistakes that result in the death of humans.

Alongside all of this, is the possibility that killer robots could go rogue. What this means is that the killer robots could advance to a point where they flat out reject their orders and create their own plans. These new "plans" do not have to be nefarious. If Japanese autonomous warships are sailing in the Indian Ocean, and are given orders to protect Japanese cargo vessels from pirates, the warships might reject this order. Instead, the warships might prefer to tail an enemy submarine that is circling the coast of Africa. How will Japan deal with its killer robots suddenly going rogue and doing whatever they want to do?

In other words, the more killer robots are used, the more intelligent they will become. Ultimately, this intelligence could backfire.

Conclusion

There is no bigger fear than killer robots turning against the world. Arguably, the same risk exists today with humans. Could hundreds of soldiers suddenly attack their superiors? Or, could a small platoon suddenly go off the map and disappear? For humans, militaries may have contingency plans if such things happen. But, do contingency plans exist for killer robots?

After all, the risk of dangerous behavior is greater with killer robots. This is because of two reasons. First, killer robots will be integrated and deployed throughout a military. And, if they all have similar or the same programming, or are all connected to the same AI-system, their behavior may mirror one another. If autonomous drones suddenly fire on friendly fighter jets with human pilots, it could mean that autonomous tanks could also fire on friendly soldiers nearby. Second, killer robots could be given superior roles, such as managing the entire cyber security infrastructure of a military (or nation), or being in charge of missile defense systems stationed on the border. And that means, even if killer robots defect or turn against humans once or twice, because of the capabilities under their control, the outcome could be deadly.

At the same time, there is a huge role that businesses will play in securing killer robots.

Manufacturing firms may keep control in case the killer robots "go rogue." Or, they may give governments a kill switch. This kill switch may only be used if absolutely necessary, considering using it may mean nations lose significant military capabilities.

There is no clear cut path to follow when it comes to managing the risks that killer robots pose to humans. And, that is because humans are essentially creating the biggest threat to their own survival and continuity. This has been the case with other weapons, like nuclear weapons. And now, this risk remerges with killer robots. Except, unlike nuclear weapons, which are under the control of humans, killer robots, by definition, will not be. Most will be completely autonomous. That raises the risk to heights never seen before.

For the first time, the fate of the human race may lie, not in the decisions humans make, but in the decisions robots make. Is humanity ready for this?

Conclusion

By now, it should be clear that the next wars and conflicts may be entirely driven, if not started, by killer robots. The human part of warfare may be completely augmented, or in some cases, may disappear entirely. As this happens, countries and companies will face challenges they have never faced with before.

What will the world do?

This book may be a starting point. Perhaps, regions of the world will join hands and develop new "regional ethics" to control how killer robots behave. Or, perhaps institutions will use killer robots to create a new role for themselves in the world. Or, perhaps, new companies may emerge, supplying killer robots to governments and groups to take advantage of a new business opportunity.

All of this, and more, is possible.

If there is one takeaway from this book, it is this: there is an infinite number of ways that killer robots could transform the world. Unfortunately, this is hard to see because most discussions around killer robots revolve around one area: killer robots taking over the world. If killer robots were a puzzle, then, right now, only one piece is being examined. Everything else is not given as much attention. This is not only wrong, it is dangerous. In the coming years, killer robots will be real, functional capabilities of many nations around the world. Countries must understand the implications of what they are acquiring and companies must understand the implications of what they are selling.

Equally important is one issue that has been left out so far. This issue is relevant to every chapter. And that is, how will killer robots affect the speed at which conflicts accelerate?

Consider that in World War 1, after the assassination of Austria's archduke, it took exactly one month for Austria to declare war on Serbia. This activated mutual defense treaties in Europe that led to a wider conflict. And, this conflict was entirely driven by humans.

If it took just one month for World War I to begin when humans were in charge, could future conflicts start in a matter of seconds or hours, when killer robots are in charge?

If a group of autonomous drones attack a plane carrying the vice-president of a nation, will this conflict accelerate faster (or slower) because killer robots are involved? The answer to this question will affect everything, from the kind of "global brains" that need to be created, to the kind of ethics that need to be integrated. If killer robots speed up conflicts, then killer robots pose an even greater risk to global peace. But, if killer robots slow down conflicts, then they may be viewed the same way cyber attacks are viewed: significant, but not worth declaring war over.

For countries and companies, institutions and investors reading this book, the focus may now be on what to do. The rest of this chapter focuses on just that. The following is a set of ideas to help the world as it grapples with the age of killer robots.

A guide to killer robot management

The biggest impact that killer robots will have is on the military capabilities of a nation. Nations will have newfound power. This is a huge transformation for nations, and a huge opportunity for companies making killer robots. For nations, the goal should be to understand how their killer robots may affect a future conflict. In the past, gauging military capabilities revolved around war games. With killer robots, governments should begin with "virtual war games." These are war games, held in virtual reality, that include killer robots. These virtual games would help soldiers coexist with killer robots, and would allow defense leaders to see, in real time, how killer robots affect a conflict, and their advantages and shortcomings. For companies selling killer robots to nations, they should build a "bridge gap." Right now, there may be gaps in the minds of nations about why they need killer robots, especially if these machines are expensive. For example, if a country in Central Europe refuses to purchase killer robots, a bridge gap may be to outsource manufacturing. This way, as the country buys killer robots, local jobs are created. Alternatively, if manufacturing cannot be shifted, the defense firm could build a lab in the country that builds "apps" for killer robots. This lab would employ locals and would jumpstart a new economy for the country. The apps would allow the killer robot to do more. This would create a new robotics and artificial intelligence (AI) ecosystem in the country that revolves around apps. In short, bridge gaps would be new, innovative ways to compel countries to buy killer robots.

The next impact that killer robots will have is that they could put countries in situations they did not want to be in. This is a huge risk for countries, and an area that killer robot makers will be forced to address. Because this is a risk, there could be a "win win" model that involves countries and companies working together. For example, as governments create new contingency plans for killer robots, they could involve killer robot companies. If a government is creating a plan for how to respond if their killer robots kill enemy soldiers, they may create a rule called "measure of blame." This rule may be created to decide whether the killer robot manufacturer should be blamed for the killer robots' behavior. One of the conditions may be around data analysis. If the killer robot did not include certain data sets when deciding whether to attack somebody, then the blame falls on the manufacturer for bad programming or wherever that "dataset" came from. It is inevitable that governments will come up with public policies and contingency plans for killer robots. And, it is in the interest of companies to work with these governments so that fair policies are created.

Another impact is that the behavior of killer robots could throw the foreign policy of a nation over the cliff. This is a huge risk for nations, as it means that their relations with other countries, or strategy to grow relations with certain countries, could be shredded. If this happens, nations might stop buying certain killer robots, a risk for manufacturers of killer robots. To stop this from happening, countries and companies may have to work together. Could companies propose that they fund new, independent and local outfits to build killer robots? This way, the killer robots will be "programmed" and built in the "language" of the country. And this way, the killer robots may think and behave in ways that align with the country's foreign policy. Alternatively, countries could mandate that firms use local AI-engineers and scientists when building killer robots. Again, this would be to influence how the killer robots think so they do not behave in rash and dangerous ways. However, these ideas do not eliminate the risk that killer robots will create problems for a country's foreign policy - they only minimize them.

An additional impact is that of future applications. Because killer robots will have several applications beyond the battlefield (such as policing), there will need to be a clear blueprint of how countries can use killer robots (and what the implications might be for society). At the same time, killer robot makers will need to decide whether they will allow countries to use killer robots in a variety of ways or whether they want to control the way their products are used. For countries, they could create a new division in their government that focuses on autonomous systems. Whether this is called the "Ministry of Algorithms" or the "Algorithmic Department," this new governmental division would set the conditions and rules for how autonomous systems, including killer robots, can be used domestically. For companies, their choices fall into two camps. First, do they allow customers to do whatever they want with a killer robot once it is sold? If so, then the transaction is black and white: the company sells the killer robot (or robots), and the country buys it (or them). But, if companies opt-in for the second choice, of controlling the killer robot once it is sold, then the transaction is not as simple. If companies choose to maintain some control, perhaps it could be over the kind of capabilities the killer robots have. For example, if a defense firm sells an autonomous drone, the "standard" operating system may be only for military missions. But, the defense firm could also sell extra packages, that allow the drone to also operate as an emergency responder or even as a transport vehicle if the drone can also carry goods and people. Over time, the defense company could come out with more and more packages, or apps, creating a new industry through expanding what killer robots can do.

The point of these ideas is not to force countries and companies to move in a certain direction. The point of these ideas is to illuminate what kind of challenges could emerge as nations deploy killer robots and how these challenges could be solved. This guide is a skeleton that can be modified and changed based on the different needs of a country or company. Equally important is that with every risk, is an equally great opportunity.

Right now, the world has not fully entered the age of killer robots. The shockwaves from killer robots have barely started, let alone reached full force. The world is still trying to understand the implications of these new war machines, let alone deploy them. But, this is a temporary phase. And, it will end very fast. In fact, it is plausible to say that many countries already have some version of killer robots but are reluctant to unveil and deploy them, for obvious reasons.

And that means, perhaps, killer robots have already started a new global conflict. Except, this conflict is not about land or resources, it is about whether or not to deploy killer robots in the first place. In this new conflict, instead of missiles and mortars, countries are using mediation and messaging.

If killer robots have already created global division before they reach the battlefield, then it may be the surest sign yet of the kind of transformation on the horizon. Except, transformation may not be the right word. Transformation is about changing the appearance or form of something. That is not all killer robots will do. For killer robots, the more apt word may be transmutation.

After all, killer robots will not just change the appearance or form of warfare, they will change warfare, period.

Key Organizations

In chronological order, the most important organizations when it comes to developing killer robots in each country:

Australia

Department of Defence
Defence Cooperative Research Center (CRC)
Defence Science and Technology Group (DST - part of Australia's Department of Defence)

Canada
Defence Research and Development Canada (DRDC)

China
Aerospace Science and Industry Intelligent Robot (ASIIR - part of of CASIC)
China Aerospace Science and Industry Corporation (CASIC)
China Electronics Technology Group (CEST)
China State Shipbuilding Corporation (CSSC)
Chinese Academy of Sciences (CAS)
National University of Defense Technology (NUDT - also referred to as the People's Liberation Army (PLA) National University of Defense Science and Technology)

Military Science Research Steering Committee (reports to Central Military Commission)

European Union

European Commission (EC)

India

Defense Research and Development Organization (DRDO)
Center for Artificial Intelligence and Robotics (CAIR, part of DRDO)

Iran

Islamic Republic of Iran Army Ground Forces (NEZAJA)
Islamic Revolution Guards Corps (IRGC)
Islamic Revolutionary Guard Corps Research and Self-Sufficiency Jihad Organization

Israel

Israeli Defense Forces (IDF)
Military Intelligence Unit (part of the Israeli Army's J6/C4i Directorates Lotem Unit)
Unit 3060 (also known as Purple unit)
Unit 8200

Procurement & Production Administration (PPD - part of Israel's Ministry of Foreign Affairs)
MANHAR
Israel Aerospace Industries (IAI)
IMI Systems (previously known as Israel Military Industries)

Japan

Acquisition, Technology & Logistics Agency (ATLA - part of the Japanese Defense Ministry)
Japanese Air Self-Defense Force (JASDF)

New Zealand

New Zealand Defence Force (NZDF)

North Atlantic Treaty Organization (NATO)

NATO Science and Technology Organization (STO)
Defense Policy and Planning Division (DPP)
Emerging Security Challenges Division (ESCD)

Russia

Foundation for Advanced Studies/Future Research Fund (FPI)
Military-Industrial Commission of the Russian Federation

Strategic Missile Forces (SMF)

Saudi Arabia

Armed Forces of Saudi Arabia
Military Industries Corporation (MIC)

Singapore

Defence Science and Technology Agency (DSTA)
DSO National Laboratories (DSO)
Singapore Armed Forces (SAF)

South Africa

South Africa National Defense Force (SANDF)

South Korea

Hanwha Group
Ministry of National Defense (MND)

Turkey

Turkish Armed Forces (TAF)

United Arab Emirates (UAE)

Dubai Police Force (DPF)

Abu Dhabi Police (ADP)
International Council on Robotics and Artificial Intelligence
Ministry of Cabinet Affairs and the Future
Minister for Artificial Intelligence

United States of America (USA)

Air Force Research Laboratory (AFRL)
Defense Advanced Research Projects Agency (DARPA)
Strategic Capabilities Office (SCO)
United States Army Tank Automotive Research, Development and Engineering Center (TARDEC)
Office of Naval Research (ONR)
Defense Innovation Unit Experimental (DIUx)
Defense Threat Reduction Agency (DTRA)
U.S. Army Research Laboratory (ARL)
Institute for Creative Technologies (ICT - part of the U.S. Army Research Laboratory)

United Kingdom (UK)

Defence Science and Technology Laboratory (DSTL)
Qinetiq (formerly part of the Defence Evaluation and Research Agency)
Industrial Strategy Challenge Fund (ISCF)
UK Research and Innovation (UKRI)

Innovation and Research Insights (IRIS) Unit

Sources

Chapter One - Rude Awakening

[1] Smith, Chris. "What Is Taranis: Everything You Need to Know about BAE Systems Unmanned Aerial Vehicle." BT.com. November 21, 2017. http://home.bt.com/tech-gadgets/future-tech/taranis-unmanned-aerial-vehicle-stealth-11364110510493.

[2] O'Hare, Ryan. "RAF Drones Could Kill without the Need for Humans." Daily Mail Online. June 10, 2016. http://www.dailymail.co.uk/sciencetech/article-3634980/RAF-drones-kill-without-need-human-operators-AI-let-machines-pick-targets-fire-will.html.

[3] "By 2030, One-Third of the IDF Ground Force Will Be Unmanned"." Israel Defense. Accessed April 23, 2019. https://www.israeldefense.co.il/en/node/31691.

[4] Markoff, John. "Fearing Bombs That Can Pick Whom to Kill." The New York Times. November 11, 2014. https://www.nytimes.com/2014/11/12/science/weapons-directed-by-robots-not-humans-raise-ethical-questions.html.

[5] Hambling, David. "Future - Why Russia Is Sending Robotic Submarines to the Arctic." BBC. November 21, 2017. http://www.bbc.com/future/story/20171121-why-russia-is-sending-robotic-submarines-to-the-arctic.

Chapter Two - Controlling The Storm

[6] Farooqui, Adnan. "U.S. Army Is Considering Automated AI Weapons." Ubergizmo. January 14, 2019. https://www.ubergizmo.com/2019/01/u-s-army-is-considering-automated-ai-weapons/.

[7] "India's Own Iron Man? DRDO Labs to Develop Military Robots for next Gen Warfare." India Today. June 09, 2013. https://www.indiatoday.in/india/north/story/india-drdo-developing-robotic-soldiers-to-replace-humans-in-warfare-166117-2013-06-09.

[8] Chen, Stephen. "China Developing Robotic Subs to Launch New Era of Sea Power." South China Morning Post. July 22, 2018. https://www.scmp.com/news/china/society/article/2156361/china-developing-unmanned-ai-submarines-launch-new-era-sea-power.

[9] Bar'el, Zvi. "Trump's 'Arab NATO' Push against Iran Comes to a Head, and He's the Biggest Obstacle." Haaretz.com. January 20, 2019. https://www.haaretz.com/middle-east-news/.premium-at-anti-iran-conference-trump-will-try-to-form-an-arab-nato-and-likely-fail-1.6851400.

[10] Cheng, Kenneth. "SAF Looks to Artificial Intelligence to Gain Punch." TODAYonline. October 28, 2016. https://www.todayonline.com/singapore/saf-looks-artificial-intelligence-gain-punch.

Chapter Three - Defense Exports 5.0

[11] "India, Japan to Introduce AI, Robotics in Defence Sector | India News - Times of India." The Times of India. January 22, 2018. https://timesofindia.indiatimes.com/india/india-japan-to-introduce-ai-robotics-in-defence-sector/articleshow/62597018.cms.

[12] "Russian Robot Policemen May Appear in Kazakhstan, Uzbekistan, China." AzerNews.az. August 21, 2018. https://www.azernews.az/region/136498.html.

[13] Tiku, Nitasha. "The Line Between Big Tech and Defense Work." Wired. May 21, 2018. https://www.wired.com/story/the-line-between-big-tech-and-defense-work/.

[14] "Announcing the New AWS Secret Region | Amazon Web Services." Amazon. November 26, 2017. https://aws.amazon.com/blogs/publicsector/announcing-the-new-aws-secret-region/.

[15] Crabtree, Justina. "Google's next A.I. Research Center Will Be in Africa." CNBC. June 14, 2018. https://www.cnbc.com/2018/06/14/google-ai-research-center-to-open-in-ghana-africa.html.

[16] "Amazon Opens Search for Amazon HQ2 – A Second Headquarters City in North America." BusinessWire. September 07, 2017. https://www.businesswire.com/news/home/20170907005717/en/Amazon-Opens-Search-Amazon-HQ2---Headquarters.

[17] Ng, Alfred. "Here's What the Final 20 Cities Offered Amazon for HQ2." CNET. January 18, 2018. https://www.cnet.com/g00/news/heres-what-the-20-finalist-cities-offered-amazon-for-hq2/?i10c.ua=1&i10c.encReferrer=aHR0cHM6Ly93d3cuZ29vZ2xlLmNvbS8=&i10c.dv=12.

[18] Russell, Jon. "Malaysia's Capital Will Adopt 'smart City' Platform from Alibaba – TechCrunch." TechCrunch. January 29, 2018. https://techcrunch.com/2018/01/29/malaysia-alibaba-city-brain/.

[19] Kahn, Jeremy. Bloomberg.com. January 20, 2019. https://www.bloomberg.com/news/articles/2019-01-20/facebook-endows-ai-ethics-institute-at-german-university-tum.

[20] Singh, Malvika. "India's Bid for the Nuclear Suppliers Group." Global Risk Insights. November 29, 2018. https://globalriskinsights.com/2018/11/indias-bid-nuclear-suppliers-group-nsg/.

[21] Gilbert, David. "Russian Weapons Maker Kalashnikov Developing Killer AI Robots." VICE News. July 12, 2017. https://news.vice.com/en_us/article/vbzq8y/russian-weapons-maker-kalashnikov-developing-killer-ai-robots.

[22] Regan, Tom. "A Russian Military Contractor Is Building Huge Drone Tanks." Engadget. March 16, 2017. https://www.engadget.com/2017/03/16/a-russian-military-contractor-is-building-huge-drone-tanks/.

[23] IBM Research Editorial Staff. "Protecting the Intellectual Property of AI with Watermarking." IBM Research Blog. July 20, 2018. https://www.ibm.com/blogs/research/2018/07/ai-watermarking/.

[24] Seidel, Jamie. "F-35 Stealth Fighter Caught Spying on Its Owners." News.Com.Au. December 2, 2017. https://www.news.com.au/technology/online/security/spy-f35s-send-sensitive-norwegian-military-data-back-to-lockheed-martin-in-the-united-states/news-story/12b4fafce6b579448cc8416518063d1f.

[25] Hambling, David. "If Drone Swarms Are the Future, China May Be Winning." Popular Mechanics. December 23, 2016. https://www.popularmechanics.com/military/research/a24494/chinese-drones-swarms/.

[26] YouTube. November 01, 2016. https://www.youtube.com/watch?v=rFrj_A1OaMw.

Chapter Four - Preparing For The Unexpected

[27] Robitzski, Dan. "Russia Is Planning a "ground Force" of Armed Military Robots." Futurism. March 21, 2019. https://futurism.com/russia-ground-force-armed-military-robots.

[28] Ayres-Deets, Andrea. "5 Of the World's Most Elite Mercenary Armies." Mic. May 8, 2013. https://mic.com/articles/40307/5-of-the-world-s-most-elite-mercenary-armies#.VCs500SHZ.

[29] Hall, Richard. "US Troops in Syria Could Be Replaced by Private Contractors, Says Blackwater Founder." The Independent. January 15, 2019. https://www.independent.co.uk/news/world/middle-east/syria-us-troop-withdrawal-private-contractors-blackwater-erik-prince-trump-military-a8729121.html.

[30] Axe, David. "Pirate-Fighters, Inc.: How Mercenaries Became Ships' Best Defense." Wired. August 23, 2011. https://www.wired.com/2011/08/pirate-fighters-inc/.

[31] Bennetts, Marc. "Families Ask Kremlin to Admit Russian Mercenaries Killed in Syria." The Guardian. February 16, 2018. https://www.theguardian.com/world/2018/feb/16/russian-mercenaries-in-syria-buried-quietly-and-forgotten.

[32] Wong, Catherine. "'Underwater Great Wall': Chinese Firm Proposes Building Network of Submarine Detectors to Boost Nation's Defence." South China Morning Post. May 19, 2016. https://www.scmp.com/news/china/diplomacy-defence/article/1947212/underwater-great-wall-chinese-firm-proposes-building.

[33] "'Underwater Great Wall' of Sensors Mooted for China." The Straits Times. May 20, 2016. https://www.straitstimes.com/world/underwater-great-wall-of-sensors-mooted-for-china.

[34] Villasanta, Arthur Dominic. "China Will Build 'Underwater Great Wall' to Cement Control over South China Sea." Chinatopix. May 30, 2017. http://www.chinatopix.com/articles/114264/20170530/china-will-build-underwater-great-wall-cement-control-over-south.htm.

Chapter Five - Global Fallout

[35] Shalal, Andrea. "World Must Keep Lethal Weapons under Human Control, Germany Says." Reuters. March 15, 2019. https://uk.reuters.com/article/uk-germany-arms-idUKKCN1QW2NR.

36 Bell, Lee. "Darpa's MIT's Eyeriss Chip Uses 'neural Networks' to Act like the Human Brain." Daily Mail Online. February 08, 2016. http://www.dailymail.co.uk/sciencetech/article-3436954/Drones-think-like-humans-heading-war-zones-Darpa-chip-uses-neural-networks-act-like-human-brain.html.

37 Huifeng, He. "Shenzhen to House Intelligent Robot Branch of China Aerospace Science and Industry Corp as Civil and Military Projects Set to Merge." South China Morning Post. March 09, 2016. http://www.scmp.com/tech/enterprises/article/1922679/shenzhen-house-intelligent-robot-branch-china-aerospace-science-and.

38 McCaney, Kevin. "AI Machines Can Think for Themselves, but Can They Explain Themselves." Defense Systems. August 11, 2016. https://defensesystems.com/articles/2016/08/11/xai-darpa-explainable-artificial-intelligence.aspx.

39 Moore, Mckenna. "UBS Digitally Cloned Its Chief Economist So He Wouldn't Miss His Meetings." Fortune. January 5, 2018. http://fortune.com/2018/07/05/ubs-digital-clone-chief-economist-daniel-kalt/.

[40] Haridy, Rich. "Real "fake News": China Introduces AI News Anchor." New Atlas. November 08, 2018. https://newatlas.com/china-ai-digital-news-anchor/57158/.

Chapter Six - Rebalancing, Rewiring

[41] Ackerman, Evan. "U.S. Army Considers Replacing Thousands of Soldiers With Robots." IEEE Spectrum: Technology, Engineering, and Science News. January 22, 2014. https://spectrum.ieee.org/automaton/robotics/military-robots/army-considers-replacing-thousands-of-soldiers-with-robots.

[42] Cox, Matthew. "Army Chief Wants Robotic Vehicles, AI for Future Battles." Military.com. January 17, 2018. https://www.military.com/defensetech/2018/01/17/army-chief-wants-robotic-vehicles-ai-future-battles.html.

[43] Rohrlich, Justin. "The US Army Wants to Turn Tanks into AI-powered Killing Machines." Quartz. February 26, 2019. https://qz.com/1558841/us-army-developing-ai-powered-autonomous-weapons/.

44 Stein, Jeff. "U.S. Military Budget Inches Closer to $1 Trillion Mark, as Concerns over Federal Deficit Grow." The Washington Post. June 19, 2018. https://www.washingtonpost.com/news/wonk/wp/2018/06/19/u-s-military-budget-inches-closer-to-1-trillion-mark-as-concerns-over-federal-deficit-grow/?noredirect=on.

45 Johnson, Jesse. "Chinese Defense Spending to Grow 7.5% in 2019 as Beijing Seeks 'world-class' Military." The Japan Times. March 5, 2019. https://www.japantimes.co.jp/news/2019/03/05/asia-pacific/politics-diplomacy-asia-pacific/chinese-defense-spending-grow-7-5-2019-beijing-seeks-world-class-military/.

46 Beng, Ben Ho Wan. "Are Aircraft Carriers Still Relevant?" The Diplomat. November 15, 2018. https://thediplomat.com/2018/11/are-aircraft-carriers-still-relevant/.

47 Macias, Amanda. "The First Drone Warship Just Joined the Navy and Now Nearly Every Element of It Is Classified." CNBC. April 25, 2018. https://www.cnbc.com/2018/04/25/first-drone-warship-joins-us-navy-nearly-every-element-classified.html.

[48] Macias, Amanda. "America's Most Expensive Weapons System Just Got a Little Cheaper." CNBC. September 28, 2018. https://www.cnbc.com/2018/09/28/f-35-fighter-jets-americas-most-expensive-weapons-system-just-got-a-little-cheaper.html.

Chapter Seven - Humanity's Last Hurrah

[49] Georgieva, Stanislava. "Russia Tests a New Onboard AI System on Mi-28N Attack Helicopter." Bulgarian Military Industry Review. February 22, 2019. https://bulgarianmilitary.com/2019/02/22/russia-tests-a-new-onboard-ai-system-on-mi-28n-attack-helicopter/.

[50] Crew, Bec. "Google's AI Has Learned to Become "Highly Aggressive" in Stressful Situations." ScienceAlert. March 31, 2018. https://www.sciencealert.com/google-deep-mind-has-learned-to-become-highly-aggressive-in-stressful-situations.

[51] Greene, Tristan. "AI Touch Myself: Scientists Create Self-replicating Neural Network." The Next Web. March 29, 2018. https://thenextweb.com/artificial-intelligence/2018/03/29/ai-touch-myself-scientists-create-self-replicating-neural-network/.

[52] Metz, Rachel. "Google's StarCraft-playing AI Is Crushing Pro Gamers." CNN. January 24, 2019. https://www.cnn.com/2019/01/24/tech/deepmind-ai-starcraft/index.html.

[53] Griffin, Andrew. "Facebook Robots Shut down after They Talk to Each Other in Language Only They Understand." The Independent. July 31, 2017. https://www.independent.co.uk/life-style/gadgets-and-tech/news/facebook-artificial-intelligence-ai-chatbot-new-language-research-openai-google-a7869706.html.

[54] Khoury, Jack. "Israeli Strikes on Syria Killed 113 Iranian Soldiers over past Month, Syrian Observatory for Human Rights Reports." Haaretz.com. September 17, 2018. https://www.haaretz.com/israel-news/.premium-israeli-strikes-on-syria-killed-113-iranian-soldiers-1.6489386.

[55] Cuthbertson, Anthony. "Sex Robots Could Be Transformed into Killers by Hackers, Security Expert Warns." Newsweek. January 1, 2018. https://www.newsweek.com/hacked-sex-robots-could-murder-people-767386.

[56] "Iran Claims It Hacked and Controlled US Drones, Shows Footage from Missions as Proof (VIDEO)." RT International. February 21, 2019. https://www.rt.com/news/452116-iran-claims-control-us-drones/.